Welcome Back!

Michael Jordan's return allows his legions of admirers to become unconditional fans once again

His name had become synonymous with creative, tongue-wagging acrobatics that resulted in three NBA MVP awards and three consecutive world championships.

Further, Michael Jordan's bald pate and toothy grin were splashed across interstate highway billboards and living room television sets throughout the continent, even after he embarked on his improbable quest to break into Major League Baseball.

When Michael "retired" from basketball at age 30, we continued to wear his shoes, clamor for his autograph, don his apparel, consume his sports drink and enjoy his story.

Everyone, it seemed, still wanted to be like Mike.

Everyone also couldn't wait to welcome him back.

Michael Jordan built himself into a

The NBA spotlight shines again on Michael Jordan.

global figure, both as a basketball player and as a pitchman, with his high-flying style, incomparable smile and peerless record of achievement.

His ferocious, competitive nature made him a winner at every level of basketball: All-State at Laney High in

Wilmington, N.C., All-American at North Carolina and All-Universe for the Chicago Bulls. And don't forget those Olympic gold medals.

When Jordan announced his return to basketball after a 17-month retirement junket on the minor league baseball circuit, pundits likened the event to the resurrection of Elvis, the reunion of the Beatles and the second coming of Babe Ruth all wrapped into one.

An exaggeration, to be sure, but in an era of sports when negativity, greed and labor impasse have frustrated us all, Jordan's return to the game he once dominated serves as a reminder of why Americans embrace their sports and idolize the great professional players.

Michael's return helped revitalize the notion that, yes, we could be unconditional fans once again.

Michael. One name is all that's needed. This is his story.

— The Editors

Publisher/Editor Dr. James Beckett
Vice President, Publishing Fred L. Reed III
Corporate Vice President Joe Galindo
Controller Claire B. Backus
Vice President, Sales Jeff Amano

Beckett® Sports Heroes: Michael Jordan
Senior Editor Gary Santaniello
Art Director Lisa McQuilkin Monaghan
Technical Advisor Rich Klein
Assistant Production Manager Barbara Barry

Staff Theresa Anderson, Jeff Anthony, Therese Bellar, Louise Bird, Jud Chappell, Tommy Collins, Kim Ford, Beth Harwell, Mark Harwell, Patti Harris, Pepper Hastings, Julia Jernigan, Jay Johnson, Rudy J. Klancnik, Jane Ann Layton, Mike Moss, Rich Olivieri, Reed Poole, Margaret Steele, Lawrence Treachler

Copyright 1995, by Dr. James Beckett
All rights reserved under International and Pan-American Copyright Conventions.
Published by: House of Collectibles, 201 East 50th Street, New York, NY 10022
Distributed by Ballantine Books, a division of Random House, Inc., New York, and simultaneously in Canada by Random House of

CONTENTS

BAS

The Prodigal

RETURNS

In fulfilling his faithful's fondest wishes by returning to the NBA, Michael Jordan has raised hopes for a reprise of hoop heaven

By Paul Ladewski

MICHAEL JORDAN

When one considers the extent of hero worship afforded one Michael Jeffrey Jordan in Chicago, not to mention global points elsewhere, perhaps it was fitting that the NBA's so-called Second Coming took on religious trappings. Indeed, prior to Jordan's long-awaited, much-debated return in Indianapolis on March 19, the Bulls' practice facility in suburban Deerfield resembled a scene outside the Vatican. For 10 days, fans and media anxiously awaited word on St. Michael of Jordan, their vigil not unlike the way the masses would hold a vigil for the next pope.

The pose for the statue unveiled outside the United Center last November was fitting, since so many of Michael's most fantastic feats occurred while he was in flight.

Michael shared many special moments with his father. After James Jordan's death in July 1993, Michael honored his memory by pursuing a baseball career.

Then, on the glorious (at least for Michael's most ardent followers) Saturday afternoon of March 18, white smoke finally appeared in the form of these simple words: "I'm back."

With that two-word statement issued through Jordan's agent, David Falk, thus returned a basketball deity. The message from Michael came 17 months after Jordan surprised — no, make that shocked — the faithful with his retirement from the game and the league he'd ruled for nine years.

To understand the stranglehold that Jordan had on the sporting public, one only had to be among the dozens present at the Berto Center on the Bulls' practice days leading up to The Comeback. On Day 5 of the Jordan Watch, a hint of Air definitely lingered in the air.

After Michael drove his black Range Rover into the players' parking lot at 9:30 a.m., he did his best to execute a back-door play into the building, only to be caught from behind by omnipresent television crews. Joe Dumars couldn't have stopped him any better.

Yo, Mike, just what are you thinking about these days?

"I'm thinking about a lot," he said with one foot in the building.

Michael speaks! News at 10.

Soon thereafter, national and local media, about 100 in number, descended on the Berto Center. The scene outside became equally crazy. Two Deerfield police cars, three uplink satellite trucks and seven microwave trucks were among the vehicles parked outside the practice facility, prompting Bulls center and former Jordan teammate Will Perdue to remark, "Just like old times. Except some people have changed stations."

Meanwhile, throughout Da City, Michaelmania thrived. On the side of one large building that overlooks an expressway in the Loop, the word "Yes" had been inserted above Jordan's image. Another billboard announced with no small trace of hope: "Michael Jordan Welcome Back."

Telephone lines to local radio talk shows hummed at a brisk rate. It seemed inquiring minds everywhere, from Carphone Bill to Tom from Tinley Park, had the same pressing question: Will he or won't he? And the same desperate answer: He'd better.

All the while, Jordan's would-be teammates seemed to embrace the idea of a new addition for the stretch drive. "He would give us hope," Steve Kerr said. "Right now, it's not unreasonable for us to think we can get past the first round of the playoffs. But with Michael here, we would believe that a championship is possible."

The incessant talk of Jordan, though, gradually frayed their nerves. After the Bulls blew a 14-point lead late in a March 11 game against the Los Angeles Lakers and lost, Pete Myers complained, "Somebody stuck a microphone in my face, and the first thing he asked about was . . . "

Michael, Michael, Michael . . .

Amid speculation that Jordan still could walk on water, it soon became obvious he was capable of something far greater in scope. Even before he ended his deafening silence, the mere thought of his possible return to hoopdom sent tremors throughout Wall Street. According to one report, the stocks of the companies Jordan endorses — Nike, Quaker Oats, General

Not So FAST

Even while his No. 23 ascended to the rafters of the United Center last November, clues hinted that the elaborate retirement ceremony for Michael may have been premature

It was billed "A Salute to Michael Jordan," but to anyone who witnessed it last November, it looked conspicuously like a special, two-hour episode of *This Is Your Life*.

Cheers from Woody Harrelson, George Wendt, Kelsey Grammer. Craig T. Nelson. Larry King, hello. Spike Lee ("Boooooo"). Robert Smigel. Boyz II Men. Bobby Knight. Dean Smith. Even Bulls general manager Jerry Krause (louder "Boooooo"). It seemed everyone except Ralph Edwards was in attendance at the United Center.

They replayed video highlights of his career. They showered him with gifts, including a golf swing analyzer and an outdoor putting green. They told very nice stories about him. They unveiled outside the United Center an 11-1/2 foot bronze sculpture of Air Jordan in flight. Yet the made-for-TV extravaganza had nothing to do with glitz and glamour and Ahmad Rashad, really. It had more to do with the fact that, in a sports world littered with holdouts and cop-outs, the star of stars had shot as straight with his public as he once did on the court.

Jordan's No. 23 reached new heights when raised to the United Center's rafters.

The festivities took place 13 months after Jordan had turned Chicago into the City of Droopy Heads with his announced retirement from basketball, soon to embark on a baseball career. At the time, it seemed just a handful of observers believed the stunning news. Even fewer wanted to. As no less an NBA expert than Sinbad pleaded for Jordan followers everywhere, "You know he's going to play one more game. You just know it."

When Rashad, a close Jordan buddy, said, "I just know he's going to play one more game," perhaps that should have been a clue to a comeback. Indeed, months later, Bulls head coach Phil Jackson revealed that when he half-jokingly mentioned a possible return to him, Jordan indicated he already had given it some serious thought.

Yet when he and his three small children raised No. 23 to the rafters in what would be the evening's most touching moment Jordan appeared to slam dunk that notion. "With that number hanging up, that puts it to rest," he said afterward. "I've got to move on. There's a new team here. I'm playing baseball."

Before the night was finished, few dry eyes could be found, and Jordan's were among them. From all appearances, this was to be his last public contact with basketball until his visit to Springfield, Mass., a few jump shots from now.

As Jordan said, "I achieved my dream in basketball. My dream now is to play baseball — Major League Baseball. I'm working toward that. The most important thing is I achieved everything I could. I chose the time to retire. I'm enjoying what I'm doing. Hopefully, the fans can enjoy the memories."

Little did anyone know at the time how soon those memories would be rekindled.   •
— *Paul Ladewski*

BILL SMITH / SPORTS ILLUSTRATED

Mills and McDonald's — gained $2.3 billion in value during the week after the hint of a comeback became public.

Once Michael's return became official, the extent of his hold on the public became apparent. NBC's telecast of the game against Indiana on March 19 attracted 35 million viewers, making it the most-watched regular season game in NBA history. This despite the fact that Jordan's return played opposite the second round of the NCAA basketball tournament.

Wearing No. 45, because his late father, James, saw the last game he played wearing his retired No. 23, Michael hit just seven of 28 shots and scored merely 19 points in Chicago's 103-96 overtime loss to the Pacers. But the important thing wasn't *how* he came back, but simply that he *was* back.

"When I decided to come back, I knew I would be out of sync," he explained after the game. "I knew there would be ups and downs."

Three games later, Jordan hit a 16-foot buzzer beater to down Atlanta. Then, in his next game, Jordan scored 55 points (the highest point total in the

Upon the stunning announcement of Michael's retirement on Oct. 6, 1993, the City of Broad Shoulders collectively slouched.

league this season) in a victory over the Knicks at Madison Square Garden. Guess those are considered "ups."

As for why he came back, Jordan says the decision boiled down to his enduring passion for basketball.

"Eventually, I just decided that I loved the game too much to stay away," he says.

On Oct. 6, 1993, a decidedly more somber scene played out at the Berto Center. Flanked by his wife, Juanita, and Bulls majority owner Jerry Reinsdorf, Jordan did the unthinkable by announcing his retirement from basketball after nine seasons, which included three Most Valuable Player awards and as many NBA championship rings. "I'm not going to make it a 'never' issue," he said that day. "I'm saying I don't have the drive right now."

On the surface, there appeared to be some legitimate reasons why Jordan's internal flame had lost its intensity. For one, the murder of his father just two months earlier had done much to rob his spirit. While Jordan claimed the sudden loss wasn't the sole reason for his decision, it certainly impressed upon him that life was more than a breakaway slam dunk. He wanted to spend more quality time with his wife and three children and away from "you guys," as he often calls the media. And, of course, there was the matter of his ever-beckoning golf clubs.

What's more, Jordan just had paced himself through a physically grueling season, one in which, at age 30, he appeared to play at a mere human level with more regularity. With the ink of a third consecutive league title still fresh on his resume, as he flatly put it, "I just feel that I don't have anything else to prove." With training camp yet to begin, the reasoning went, this was as good a time as any for Bulls teammates and management to come to grips with life after Michael.

Even so, Jordan's farewell remained cloaked in mystery, at least a trace of which remains even today. On this darkest of days in Chicago, the emotional figure who danced on a scorer's table after the league championship clincher just two years previous seemed remarkably calm, almost without emotion. The lack of finality in Jordan's voice seemed to leave the door wide open for another jump shot in future years. Indeed, few who had witnessed

Michael returned for the last game at Chicago Stadium when he played in Scottie Pippen's charity game. Leaving the hardwood, he kissed the Bulls' logo on the floor in a farewell salute to an old friend.

The sign outside the United Center signaled the sentiments of Michael's adopted city when Jordan announced his return to basketball.

His jump shot may have been rusty in his first game back after a 21-month hiatus from NBA action, but before long Jordan had demonstrated his deadly scoring touch of old.

Jordan's competitive fire and understood his love for the game believed the so-called retirement would amount to anything more than a much-publicized leave of absence.

The question was, why now? Sure, Jordan no longer was his dominant self at times, but he wasn't exactly an embarrassment, either. The fact was, when His Airness absolutely had to be at his tongue-wagging best, his elevator still stopped at more floors than anybody else's in the game. And he just had lit up the Phoenix Suns for a record 41 points per game in the recently concluded NBA Finals. Plus, with a nucleus of B.J. Armstrong, Horace Grant and Scottie Pippen around him, more championships were in the offering, weren't there? To more than a few observers, his didn't appear to be classic symptoms of basketball burnout.

An ongoing investigation into Jordan's gambling activities cast a black cloud over the episode. Only days after the retirement announcement, Commissioner David Stern called off the dogs, saying the league had uncovered no serious wrongdoings. Yet critics maintained the matter had been conveniently swept under the rug, which coupled with Jordan's retirement, aimed to cool potentially harmful talk. This much is certain: If the league was deathly afraid of a full-blown, Pete Rose-type controversy, nobody seems to know for sure. And maybe we never will.

Much more certain was the impact of Jordan's exit on his so-called supporting cast. The consensus was that, now that the Air had been taken out of them, the Bulls immediately would crash and burn. For the better part of three weeks at the beginning of the 1993-94 campaign, those predictions rang true. Chicago opened with seven losses in 11 games.

Just when the Bulls appeared headed for a rare season from hell, who should burst upon the scene but Scottie Pippen. For years, Pippen had played Tonto to Jordan's Lone Ranger, resigned forever to do his many splendid things in relative anonymity. Suddenly, out from underneath the NBA's largest shadow, Pippen became the obvious choice to carry the torch as the club's best player and veteran leader.

On one of two counts, at least, the All-Star forward delivered in a big way. Led by Pippen, Armstrong, Grant and the usual role players, the Bulls became one of the surprises of the regular season, compiling a 55-27 record. After an obligatory victory against Cleveland in the first round of the playoffs, the Bulls extended New York to seven games before they succumbed to the Knicks' depth, muscle and homecourt advantage.

As it turned out, the biggest void that Jordan's retirement created was that of veteran leadership. Pippen, the obvious choice to become the voice of reason, never felt truly comfortable in this role, and the longer the season wore on, the more his uneasiness about it showed. The situation came to a head at the most crucial of times, in Game 3 against the Knicks, when Pippen staged his infamous sitdown strike with 1.8 seconds left in the game. While the Bulls managed to win the game on a buzzer-beating shot by Toni Kukoc, the incident had set the tone for the remainder of the series. Certainly, one could make a case that, with the calming effect of a certain saintly shooting guard, the Bulls would have advanced to the NBA Finals, at the very least.

Now, nearly two years later, Michael is in position to lead his people back to the promised land. •

Paul Ladewski covers the Bulls for the Chicago Daily Southtown.

HOME again

The circumstances surrounding Michael's Chicago homecoming and first game in the United Center made for an electric atmosphere

The anticipation began the previous Saturday, when he announced he again would be a pro basketball player. In the six days leading up to Michael Jordan's first game in the United Center, it gathered fury like the rolling thunder that follows a flash of lightning.

The circumstances of the event suggested stage management by a power greater than even David Stern or Nike. Orlando, owner of the league's best record and boasting Jordan's successor as the NBA's top draw (Shaquille O'Neal) and his stylistic heir (Anfernee Hardaway), provided the competition. All standing room tickets were sold, promising an attendance in excess of 23,000. A media onslaught five times the turnout for a typical game, coupled with a national cable television audience in prime time, created a supercharged atmosphere.

The new building buzzed well in advance of the tip-off. Fans of all types waved celebratory placards distributed by both Chicago dailies and various companies connected to His Airness. Michael's entrance onto the United Center hardwood was greeted with thunderous noise, which echoed every time he made a layup during pregame drills.

The climax came as his name was called at the conclusion of the Bulls' player introductions — "from North Carolina . . ."

At that moment, where the fulfillment of the fans' most fervent wishes collided with the promise of magical days ahead, nothing seemed impossible. Despite a subpar performance from an admittedly anxious Jordan, for the first time in 17 months all felt right in Chicagoland and many points beyond. The Jordan faithful again had a reason to believe. •

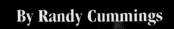

By Randy Cummings

Good A

Michael's 55-point outburst against the Knicks five games into his comeback served notice that his skills still pack potency. What else can fans expect from *Jordan, The Sequel?*

Ever?

Once it has been relegated to the history books, long after the ink has dried, his story will be read in a straightforward manner.

Michael Jordan, the greatest basketball player ever to lace up sneakers, retires from the game in his prime. A three-time NBA champion, he has nothing left to prove and no room left in his trophy case.

Then, he briefly chases his own field of dreams with a bat and glove.

Seventeen months later, Michael Jordan — we mentioned him being the greatest basketball player ever, right? — returns to the hardwood.

Simple, huh?

Upstaging the 1994 NCAA tournament with his own version of March Madness, Jordan teased the world — yes, the world breathlessly awaited his decision — with a few appearances at Chicago Bulls practices. Then on March 18, he issued a simple, two-word statement: "I'm back."

Of course, getting His Airness back in his familiar red-and-white uniform, this time in No. 45 instead of his retired No. 23 that hangs from the United Center rafters, hardly was easy. Far from it.

But for all the wondering and waiting and, in the case of basketball fans everywhere, dreaming, Jordan's return to the game he so eloquently had dominated was worth the wait.

When he stepped back into the national spotlight on March 19 against the Indiana Pacers in front of a national NBC audience, the rust that had accumulated around the edges of his game — he connected on seven of 28 field goals for 19 points in a Bulls' overtime loss — was overlooked for the pure joy of having him back with us. Wagging tongue and all.

"I'm only back for the love of the game," he told the cameras.

"They weren't the greatest highlights, but I'm glad to be back."

WHY JORDAN came back, of course, will be a long-standing topic of debate and another chapter for his ever-growing entry into those history books.

The most logical answer, as he stated, points to an affection for the game that apparently was too overpowering to ignore. He's played basketball and dominated it for so long — and it's brought all of what his life is today — that he wanted it to become a part of his life again.

Just maybe, he missed it.

When sport's greatest comeback since Muhammad Ali's three-year exile from boxing for resisting the draft in the 1960s finally became a reality, Jordan naturally faced being measured against his own incredible standards. But, hey, what better motivation for the ultimate competitor?

If he, indeed, was the best player ever when he retired, it only goes to reason that he believes he can push himself to that lofty status once again. Don't expect him to either worry about or allow his image to become tarnished by a less-than-worthy comeback effort.

Beyond the personal quest boiling within Jordan, external forces also drive him. Mainly, his presence in a Chicago uniform not only will have a tremendous effect on the Bulls, but it will affect the entire Eastern Conference. The Bulls were a playoff team before his arrival, but with a Michael Jordan in the lineup, their postseason outlook brightens considerably.

"[Jordan's return] puts Chicago right back into the championship playoff picture," broadcaster and Hall

Plenty of good basketball lays ahead for Jordan, considering he's yet to fully exploit the shorter three-point arc and the tighter restrictions on hand-checking.

JACK NICHOLSON BLASTS LETTERMAN'S OSCAR SKIT
Nicholson
Neal Travis exclusive: Page 3

PRETTY WOMAN DITCHES LYLE
Lovett and Roberts
See Page 5

NEW YORK POST
LATE CITY FINAL
WEDNESDAY, MARCH 29, 1995 / sunny today, 55; increasing clouds tonight, 40 / Details, Page 16 ● ● R   50¢

MIRACLE MAN
Air Jordan storms Garden with 55 points
Pages 56 59

Michael Jordan soars over Anthony Mason on his return to the Apple last night. The Bulls edged the Knicks 113-111

Demonstrating that his flair for the dramatic remains exquisite, Michael confirmed his comeback with a 55-point explosion ideally suited for the next day's tabloids.

Although Scottie Pippen is one of just three who remain from the starting unit Michael left behind, Chicago again is bullish on the prospect of a fourth NBA title.

of Famer Bill Walton predicts.

Of course, times change and not all was the same with the Bulls when Jordan rejoined them. Just three members of the current team (Scottie Pippen, B.J. Armstrong and Will Perdue) were around when the Jordan-led Bulls three-peated championships in 1991, 1992 and 1993. So, in addition to pushing himself to play up to the level he attained before he left, Jordan also shoulders the enormous burden of being expected to carry the Bulls back to the NBA Finals again.

But since he did it before — more precisely, *three* times before — who's to say he won't do it again?

"The biggest thing for me is not to change this team, but to try to fit in," Jordan says. "They were doing very well during the last 18 months. I just want to add to that and make them a little more dangerous."

IF MICHAEL needs to look beyond the Bulls for inspiration, there are several new, young opponents out there who never have had the chance to give him their best shot — or, as frequently was the case with earlier challengers — be embarrassed by him.

Exciting new one-on-one matchups that could rival his highlight-worthy duels with the Pistons' Joe Dumars, the Knicks' John Starks and the Pacers' Reggie Miller are just

waiting to make headlines in 1995-96. Remember, Michael was busy in a batting cage somewhere when potential rivals such as Grant Hill, Glenn Robinson, Anfernee Hardaway and Isaiah Rider arrived on the NBA scene.

Although his first couple of games displayed a Jordan who winded easily, operated on tired legs and exhibited a shooting eye that still was a little off, it wasn't long — five games, to be exact — before the Jordan of old returned.

In Michael's second game, a final visit to Boston Garden, Michael stirred memories by scoring 27 points in 26 minutes, hitting nine of the 17 field goals and knocking down all eight

— was there *really* any doubt? — disappeared permanently three nights later in New York. In just his fifth game since coming back, Jordan outdid . . . Jordan.

Looking every bit the unstoppable scoring machine of days gone by, Jordan exploded for 55 points — and dished a game-winning assist to Bill Wennington, whose last-second dunk gave Chicago a 113-111 victory — against the Knicks. His brilliant performance ("We have Superman on our team," joked Bulls guard Steve Kerr) established a new Madison Square Garden single-game record against the Knicks. His record surpassed the previous mark held by, you guessed it, himself.

"I'm starting to get the hang of this," Michael told reporters afterward. "It was, well, just like old times."

As it turned out, Indiana Pacers head coach Larry Brown was right. Jordan's impact was almost immediate.

"He could step off a flight from Japan at midnight, check into a hotel, change clothes and help you win a championship if you needed it that night," Brown predicted to *USA Today* before Jordan announced his return.

As if he needed any help, Michael's personal quest to get his game back in shape probably will be aided by two rule changes. First, Jordan should be able to take advantage of the elimination of hand checking as a defensive tactic, which could allow him to drive more easily to the basket or result in him getting fouled more often.

The Jordan of yesteryear led the league twice in free throws made, and in 1986-87 he topped the league with 972 free-throw attempts. It's conceivable that next season, when he's got a full season to take advantage of the no hand-check rule, his trips to the line (where he's a career 85 percent shooter) could exceed 1,000.

Also, the NBA's three-point line has been shortened to 22 feet (21 inches closer than before), which is perfectly suited for Jordan's shooting range. Again, once he gets accustomed to the shorter arc, Jordan is a good candidate to make a mockery of it and blow away his best effort (38 percent in 1989-90) from the longer distance.

As Lakers head coach Del Harris told *USA Today*, "He was so good anyway. How can you be better than the best?"

If you're Michael Jordan, just about anything is possible. It's that simple.   •

Randy Cummings is an associate editor for Beckett Publications.

of the free throws he attempted.

Three days later, after a disappointing home debut at the new United Center the previous night, Jordan bounced back with a vintage performance on the road against the Hawks. Logging 43 minutes of action, Michael finished with 32 points and applied the finishing touch by nailing a 16-foot jumper at the buzzer in Chicago's 99-98 victory.

"I've been struggling, and I've been wanting to be successful," he said later. "I guess this is the first true sign of being productive."

Any doubt of his ability to return to his legendary form

on air

Michael's return to basketball elicited comments from a wide range of people — himself included. Here's a sampling:

"I've got three words: Thank you, baseball." — *Bulls center Will Perdue*

"He's still got all of his stuff. I'm sure conditioning is going to be a problem for him for a game or two. But once he gets in the rhythm — oh, my goodness." — *Pacers guard Reggie Miller after Jordan's first game*

"He's like a poltergeist. He's an incident by himself. He's the best already this year, even though he hasn't played a game." — Spurs forward Chuck Person

"I tried to stay away as much as I could. But when you love something so long and you walk away from it, you can only stay away so long. I missed my friends and my teammates." — *Michael Jordan*

"I hoped for it. I never thought it would be actuality." — Bulls head coach Phil Jackson

"I feel a little sorry for him. I wouldn't want to be under all that pressure. All the blame and glory will be on his shoulders." — *Bulls guard Steve Kerr*

"I'm only back for the love of the game. I'm not here for the money. I'm not here for the attention." — Michael Jordan

"There's no question he's one of the most exciting players ever, and he's young enough that he should still have some exciting years left in him. It's certainly good for the league to have one of the greatest athletes . . . back when he's still in his prime. The public does have an incredible interest in him, and that carries over into interest in our game." — *NBA deputy commissioner Russ Granik*

"It's great for the game, and it's great for the NBA. I'm excited. I think Michael will raise the level of play of everybody." — Suns guard Danny Ainge

"I think it's great. He'll come back real good because he's young and he's in shape. He won't have lost it in the time he was away." — Atlanta head coach Lenny Wilkens

"From our standpoint, it's great. The people who are suffering are probably the teams in the East. I'll be excited. Something like this can't come every day." — Suns guard Kevin Johnson

"Michael would never come back unless he felt he was absolutely ready. And Michael would be the best judge of that. No one knows his body better than he does." — Bulls vice president of basketball operations Jerry Krause

"A lot of us are excited. We hoped he would do it last year, but he didn't have the opportunity. It'll be neat." — Bulls center Bill Wennington

"It puts Chicago right up there in terms of one of the leaders now. They've been competitive; they've basically hovered around .500. With Michael Jordan, you're talking about a .700, .800 basketball team now." — Pistons head coach Don Chaney

"The Beatles and Elvis are back. It's a significant day." — Pacers head coach Larry Brown

"It was like a playoff game, but it is Mike. Everybody wants to see him." — Pacers guard Vern Fleming

STEVE LIPOFSKY

MEASURE OF GREATNESS

Michael Jordan will go down in history as the world's greatest athlete and most recognized face. But is he the best basketball player of all time?

By Kent McDill

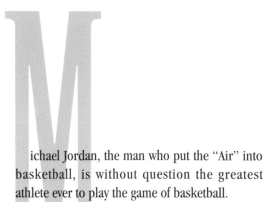

ichael Jordan, the man who put the "Air" into basketball, is without question the greatest athlete ever to play the game of basketball.

Is he, however, the greatest basketball player of all time?

The distinction is a tricky one, and one that sparked Jordan's considerable drive during his nine-season joyride through the NBA.

Now that he's back, albeit with a new number and some calluses from the batting cage, the debate again heats up. While the deep thinkers in the game try to shrug it off as apples vs. oranges, the mainstream fans have grown up watching the world's most famous tongue demand an answer.

Was Michael Jordan the greatest basketball player of all time?

Let's get the numbers out of the way first. Numbers, after all, can be used to prove just about anything in sports, and they will prove here that Jordan was the best.

In the year of his 30th birthday, 1993, Jordan won the NBA scoring title for the seventh consecutive season. His average of 32.6 points per game not only was almost three points per game better than No. 2 Dominique Wilkins of Atlanta; it was better than Michael's scoring averages of the two previous seasons. Jordan finished his career with 21,541 points in regular season play (ranked 15th all time) and a career average of 32.3 points per game (ranked No. 1).

Considering Michael couldn't take a much-deserved summer break after the '91-92 campaign — because of his Dream Team commitments — his final pre-baseball campaign might go down as his finest ever.

• Jordan led the NBA in steals for the third time in his career.

• He paced all vote-getters for the All-Star Game for the seventh consecutive season, proof of his immense popularity among the fans.

NATHANIEL S. BUTLER / NBA PHOTOS

Airing It Out

"I used to think that Michael Jordan was the Babe Ruth of basketball. I have now come to believe that Babe Ruth was the Michael Jordan of baseball."
— Chicago Bulls owner Jerry Reinsdorf

Just ask former Cavs guard Craig Ehlo about Jordan's mountain-top elevation. When everyone else is coming down, Michael is still going up. His game winner over Ehlo in the first round of the 1989 playoffs is one of Jordan's most memorable moments.

• He was named the league's Most Valuable Player three times.

• As his Bulls won their third consecutive NBA crown, he was named the NBA Finals MVP for the third straight season, the only player ever to win that designation in consecutive seasons.

Jordan rewrote the NBA record books. Before he shocked the world with his retirement announcement just days before training camp, Jordan was on track to own most of the league's all-time marks, including Kareem Abdul-Jabbar's scoring record of 38,387.

Did he already do enough in his first nine seasons to be considered the best player ever? Or does he need more? Questions remain.

On Jan. 8, 1993, Jordan scored his 20,000th career point in his 620th regular season game. That was the second-fastest run to 20,000 in NBA history, behind Wilt Chamberlain's 499 games.

It was a familiar scene. Jordan finished second to Chamberlain in the historical scoring race time and time again. In a bizarre twist of scheduling fate, Jordan scored his 5,000th, 10,000th and 15,000th career points in Philadelphia and each time finished well behind the blistering pace established by Chamberlain.

The two scoring machines finished in a

dead heat for consecutive scoring crowns. Chamberlain, who once averaged an amazing 50.4 points in a season, had his streak ended by Rick Barry in 1967. Jordan ended his at a press conference Oct. 6.

Chamberlain played 14 seasons, won two world titles and averaged 30.1 points per season. However, if it hadn't been for two disappointing final seasons with the Los Angeles Lakers — when Wilt averaged less than 20 points a game — his lifetime scoring average could have been out of anyone's grasp, even Michael's. Jordan never averaged less than 20 points a game for a season. The mere thought caused him to call it quits while at the top of his profession.

When the debate about the greatest player in the game comes around at the corner tavern, the names raised will be those of Chamberlain and Jordan. Oscar Robertson will get a vote from a short guy in the crowd, and someone will suggest the names of Bill Russell, Jerry West, Kareem, Magic Johnson and Larry Bird *(please see related chart, page 29)*. But the final votes probably will be split between Wilt the Stilt and His Airness.

omeone once said statistics are for losers, so let's raise the level of debate to a higher plane.

Simply put, Michael Jordan entered the NBA capable of doing things with his body, basketball in hand, that no other basketball player ever had done. Not only could he leap in a manner never before seen, he was capable of twists and turns, shimmys and shakes — the proverbial moves that cannot be described, cannot be believed and cannot be duplicated.

"My game is such that creativity is always going to be a part of it," Jordan once said. "But it just happens. It's not something I plan. It was something I was taught very early in my career: to go out and try to please the crowd."

His one-of-a-kind offensive skills overshadow his defensive prowess, but Michael is considered one of the game's all-time best ball thieves.

Airing It Out

"No one else was that type of player and had that kind of flair. I've always been in awe of his talent on the court, and I'm even more in awe of him as a man off the court."
— future Hall of Famer Magic Johnson

Michael took the dunking of Dr. J, Julius Erving, to new heights. Comparisons were made to dancer Mikhail Baryshnikov as Jordan pirouetted past defenders both short and tall

Jordan could never explain what he did, the true mark of genius.

And he never stopped being amazing. In his first championship season, playing against the L.A. Lakers, Jordan made a dribble move to the basket and, in midair, switched the ball from one hand to the other to find an opening for a layup on the left side of the basket, when no opening existed on the right.

"Larry Bird and I were two of the smartest players you'll ever see," Magic Johnson says. "But Michael could do things on the court that we could barely imagine. Even if he had a bad game and went 1-for-10, which was rare, that one shot might be the most amazing move you've ever seen.

"In terms of excitement he creates, Michael Jordan was the greatest player who ever laced on a pair of sneakers," Johnson adds. "The players

BRIAN SPURLOCK

enjoyed watching him just as much as the fans."

Remarkably, Chamberlain seemed somewhat offended by Jordan's athletic displays.

"The more you can turn a simple play into something acrobatic, the more the fans like it," Chamberlain snipes. "Fans don't care if you're 10 points down and you should be conserving that energy to get back on defense, and apparently, neither do the players.

"But just because the fan has accepted a different style of play doesn't mean that today's athlete is a better athlete than his predecessor," Chamberlain maintains. "The guys I played with could do all of the things the guys are doing today. I could have done 360 [fancy] dunks myself. But I wasn't into showing off. Believe me, 20 years ago, Michael Jordan would not have been allowed to do the things he's doing now."

Again, that's debatable.

Jordan grew up wanting to become a star on the diamond. He fulfilled a childhood dream one summer when he took batting practice at Comiskey Park. Of course, that was simply a sneak preview of Michael's year and a half full-time quest for baseball glory.

At the time, everyone was high on Jordan's baseball skills. It didn't take long before that tune changed once Michael donned a White Sox

Airing It Out
"I can remember a time when I was watching him on TV, and then to be on the same court as him was a great feeling. He's great. All the things you see him do on TV, jumping on one side of the lane, ending up on the other side of the lane, it's for real. I think he scored 64 points on us. So he's the best in the world, and I'm gonna miss him."
— Orlando Magic center Shaquille O'Neal

minor league uniform.

"He could actually play anywhere," says former New York Yankees shortstop Tony Kubek, who once listed Jordan as his center fielder for a baseball team made up of NBA stars.

"He recognized the movement of the fastball," says Dave LaRoche, the former White Sox coach who pitched to him at the time. "It was exciting to see him do something and not be afraid to be embarrassed. There are no adjectives left to describe his ability."

Again, however, his athleticism argues to the point that Jordan is the greatest athlete ever to play the game of basketball. It does not argue the point that he was the greatest basketball player of all time.

After watching Jordan play basketball in hundreds and hundreds of games, one got the sense that, when he chose to do so, he determined the outcome of the game all by himself. When he really wanted to win a game in which the sides were relatively equal, he could, just by deciding that was the way it would be.

It is the same determination that helped Magic and Bird dominate the NBA through the 1980s.

"He does whatever it takes to get up for a game," said Phoenix head coach Paul Westphal during the 1993 NBA Finals. "He's the greatest player of all time, and he doesn't have many big games that he's played in where he's not satisfied with his performance."

There were times when that unbending

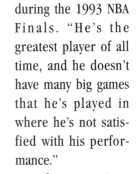

Michael didn't take long to warm up to his new surroundings in Chicago. He won the league's Rookie of the Year Award and carried the talent-thin Bulls into the playoffs.

NAME (SEASONS)	G	FG %	FT %	REB.	AST.	STL.	BLK.	PTS.	AVG.
KAREEM ABDUL-JABBAR ('69-89)	1,560	.559	.721	17,440	5,660	1,160	3,189	38,387	24.6
Championship Teams: '71, '80, '82, '85, '87, '88					Rookie Card: '69-70 Topps #25				
*RICK BARRY ('65-80)	794	.449	.900	5,168	4,017	1,104	269	18,395	23.2
Championship Teams: '75					Rookie Card: '71-72 Topps #170				
LARRY BIRD ('79-92)	897	.496	.886	8,974	5,695	1,556	755	21,791	24.3
Championship Teams: '81, '84, '86					Rookie Card: '80-81 Topps #6				
WILT CHAMBERLAIN ('59-73)	1,045	.540	.511	23,924	4,643	na	na	31,419	30.1
Championship Teams: '67, '72					Rookie Card: '61-62 Fleer #8				
BOB COUSY ('50-70)	924	.375	.803	4,786	6,955	na	na	16,960	18.4
Championship Teams: '57, '59-63					Rookie Card: '57-58 Topps #17				
*JULIUS ERVING ('76-87)	836	.507	.777	5,601	3,224	1,508	1,293	18,364	22.0
Championship Teams: '83					Rookie Card: '72-73 Topps #195				
JOHN HAVLICEK ('63-78)	1,270	.439	.815	8,007	6,114	476	117	26,395	20.8
Championship Teams: '63-66, '68, '69, '74, '76					Rookie Card: '69-70 Topps #20				
ELVIN HAYES ('69-84)	1,303	.452	.670	16,279	2,398	864	1,771	27,313	21.0
Championship Teams: '78					Rookie Card: '69-70 Topps #75				
MAGIC JOHNSON ('79-92)	874	.521	.848	6,376	9,921	1,698	361	17,239	19.7
Championship Teams: '80, '82, '85, '87, '88					Rookie Card: '80-81 Topps #6				
MICHAEL JORDAN ('84-93)	667	.516	.846	4,219	3,935	1,815	684	21,541	32.3
Championship Teams: '91, '92, '93					Rookie Card: '86-87 Fleer #57				
OSCAR ROBERTSON ('60-74)	1,040	.485	.838	7,804	9,887	na	na	26,710	25.7
Championship Teams: '71					Rookie Card: '61-62 Fleer #36				
BILL RUSSELL ('56-69)	963	.440	.561	21,620	4,100	na	na	14,522	15.1
Championship Teams: '57, '59-66, '68					Rookie Card: '57-58 Topps #77				
JERRY WEST ('60-74)	932	.474	.814	5,376	6,238	na	na	25,192	27.0
Championship Teams: '72					Rookie Card: '61-62 Fleer #43				

na: These stats weren't kept during player's era

* Does not include ABA statistics

WALTER IOOSS JR.

The best ever? Wilt has a strong case.

focus to win got in the way of the team concept of basketball. But more often than not, the team won the game and Bulls fans walked away with smiles on their faces.

"With Michael Jordan, you must step above everybody else, because he's got such a will to win," Bulls head coach Phil Jackson says.

Such a will to win could transform a lesser physical specimen — say, a Joe Montana in football — into a dramatic storybook figure.

"Jordan is what happens when the best pure athlete also happens to be the fiercest competitor in a particular sport," says George Irvine, an assistant coach with the Indiana Pacers. "I really believe that when we look back at basketball 100 years from now, he'll be seen as the greatest player ever to play the game at any position."

Airing It Out

"Michael Jordan is the only person in the entire world that I've ever met who is as competitive as I am."
— Phoenix Suns forward Charles Barkley

When Jordan entered the NBA, he was a leaper, a speedster, a magician. But he had limitations.

Early in his career, he scored a majority of his points on moves to the inside, proving to one and all that he had no fear. What we didn't know was that he was a tad gun-shy with his jumper.

So he worked on that, shooting hundreds of shots a day to perfect his range from every spot on the floor. During his three-peat run, Jordan seemed a sure bet anytime the ball left his hands, regardless of the distance or angle.

When Jordan canned that buzzer-beating

Voted to the All-Star squad starting lineup each of his nine seasons in the league, Jordan always gave fans their moneys' worth in that midseason shootout.

jumper from the top of the key against Cleveland in the fifth and final game of the 1989 playoff series, he cemented his identity as an extraordinary clutch shooter. When he drilled six three-pointers in Game 1 of the 1992 NBA Finals against Portland, he demonstrated again that his arsenal no longer was limited to highlight-film dunks.

Magic, a 6-9 point guard, wrote his Hall of Fame script with a devastating and nearly indefensible post move. Michael, who stands 6-6, tore a page out of Magic's book in adding yet another exclamation point to his own.

"Perhaps the most overlooked of Jordan's many skills was his play in the post," former Bulls head coach Doug Collins explains. "He was not only Chicago's biggest weapon down low, but he was one of the biggest in the league, as well."

"If I feel I'm not hitting my jumper, I turn around and start backing in," Jordan explained during his final season. "It's just an adjustment to the way people play me."

Making adjustments was what Jordan's game was all about. In 1987-88, when Michael grew tired of hearing the critics claim he was a one-dimensional player, he made a conscious decision to improve his defense. He produced a career-high 259 steals in 82 games (3.16 per game) and blocked a career-high 131 shots, earning his first and only Defensive Player of the Year Award.

"Today, Michael's the best offensive and defensive player we have in this league," Suns point guard Kevin Johnson said during the '92-93 Finals. "He does it all and he does it all better than anyone else."

Jordan's supreme leaping ability also enabled him to rebound with the trees of the league. He averaged a career-high eight rebounds in 1988-89 and chalked up a 6.3 per game career rebounding mark.

Like Magic and Bird before him, Jordan discovered how to bring his teammates into the picture. Perfect passes, spectacular no-look deliveries and wraparound gems helped turn Scottie

ANDREW D. BERNSTEIN / NBA PHOTOS

Airing It Out

"I found myself just wanting to stop and watch him . . . and I was playing."

— former Chicago Bulls teammate John Paxson

Pippen, Horace Grant and B.J. Armstrong into stars. Add the assist to Michael's repertoire.

Shooting, rebounding, steals, defense, assists. Jordan's game seems all-around, doesn't it?

"I'd pay money to see him practice," NBA journeyman coach Larry Brown once said.

"I don't think we'll see another player like him," Cleveland forward John Williams adds. "He is probably the world's greatest athlete."

We already know that. But what is the final answer to our "best-ever basketball player" inquiry? Do we vote for Chamberlain, the 7-1 skyscraper of intimidation and the owner of the 100-point game? Or does Michael win out in the end?

Well, let's just say we'll leave it up in the Air. •

Kent McDill covers the Bulls for the Daily Herald *in Arlington Heights, Ill.*

R ight before the 1993-94 season tipped off, Michael Jordan asked Chicago Bulls head coach Phil Jackson if there was anything left for him to accomplish as a basketball player?

For the next few seconds, there was silence.

"That's all I needed. If there was anything, he would have told me real quickly," Jordan said.

So ended the career of the world's most famous athlete.

Michael Jordan's retirement at the age of 30 sent shock waves through not only the sports world but also through the real world. This was a man whose tremendous gifts as a basketball player actually had become secondary to his immense popularity off the court. Just about everyone on the planet remains on a first-name basis with Michael.

Someday, Jordan may return to the spotlight. He definitely didn't rule out such a possibility during his farewell press conference. But for now anyway, No. 23 has walked off center stage to live, as he put it, a regular life.

So few athletes could quit cold turkey a game they so convincingly dominated. More often than not, Father Time signals the end of sports careers. Michael would never let that occur. He wanted to leave on his own terms. On Oct. 6, 1993, he said goodbye.

his final point

•

Michael Jordan scored more than 21,000 points during his nine-season NBA career. But the point he made by leaving the game while at his playing peak may be his most enduring.

"I've always stressed to people who have known me that when I lost the motivation to prove something as a basketball player, that it was time for me to move on.

"When I got to the pinnacle of my career, I'd achieved everything I could from an individual standpoint and a team standpoint. Very few people do that. I'm just happy I'm in the position to go out on top.

"I know kids will be disappointed. I hope they will understand that Michael Jordan was once a basketball player, now he's a human being and has other things he must achieve.

"I'm still in love with the game, but at some point in everyone's life you must make a decision to move forward away from games. I feel fortunate I can make that choice now.

"There's still a lot I have to do. There's a lot of family I haven't spent time with because I have been selfish with my career. It's time for me to spend time with them, with my friends. It's time to get back to a normal life, or as close to normal as I can."

•

JONATHAN DANIEL / ALLSPORT USA

Michael scored his final official points on a driving layup with 38.1 seconds left in Game 6 of the 1992-93 NBA Finals. He made his most remarkable move four months later when he announced his retirement.

rarefied AIR

Michael Jordan's flight path
to immortality wasn't clear until he embraced the NBA's
most cherished prize

i**t's funny to think about now, but just a little more than five years** ago, Michael Jordan was being mentioned in the same sentence with Ernie Banks and John Elway. He was the greatest athlete *never* to play for a championship team.

Oh, there was a national championship at North Carolina in 1982, and a gold medal at the 1984 Olympics, both of which he played significant roles in winning. But until the Chicago Bulls — Jordan's team — broke through and won it all, No. 23 was destined to go down in history as the game's finest "individual" talent. To a player like Mike, a player who treats practice games like Game 7 of the NBA Finals, this was a label he desperately wanted to shed.

When the Bulls rolled over the Los Angeles Lakers in the 1990-91 Finals, Jordan didn't even try to fight back the tears of happiness.

They christened the trophy he'd battled so hard to hold. Obviously, after claiming two more trophies and another gold medal, Michael officially can trash his one-dimensional label and stamp "WINNER" on his glowing resume. Now, he can join big-time winners such as Magic Johnson, Larry Bird, Bill Russell and Bob Cousy in the NBA's most elite fraternity.

But for what Jordan did in his final three full-time seasons, a new club should be formed. Membership: One. The Bulls three-peated, a feat not even the Magic Man or Larry Legend can boast about. Jordan won all three MVP awards, something no other player ever has done. And Michael did all of this while held under the brightest spotlight of any athlete — maybe any person — in the world.

Three NBA beat writers who held front-row seats for Michael's meteoric ride to the winner's circle detail each stop.

finding the CURE

1990-91 NBA Finals
Bulls 4, Lakers 1

BY KENT McDILL **a** generation before Michael Jordan dunked for the first time in Chicago, Ernie Banks finished his baseball career with the Cubs. That career included 512 home runs, two league MVP awards, a Hall of Fame plaque and exactly zero World Series appearances.

Suddenly, Chicago had a new catchphrase for its best athletes. The Ernie Banks Syndrome it was called, and it came to describe any star player unable to achieve ultimate team success.

For six seasons, Jordan suffered under the yoke of the Ernie Banks Syndrome.

Not that he was the first. Walter Payton of the Chicago Bears bore that stigma until his next-to-last season, by which time he was almost a footnote in the Bears' offensive scheme.

After his 1984 arrival in Chicago, Jordan carried the Bulls to the playoffs every season. But never had they ventured to the Finals. By the 1990-91 season, the yoke once worn by Payton had been transferred to the neck of Jordan, the NBA's most exciting player and easily its best athlete.

Jordan turned 28 during the '90-91 season and had played all but one regular season game during the previous four campaigns. If he was going to lift the Bulls to a world title, he was going to have to do it soon. There was no question about Jordan's athletic abilities. He had claimed scoring titles, dunk crowns and All-Star Game appearances. The question was whether he was a team player, as Magic Johnson and Larry Bird proved themselves to be throughout the 1980s.

After Chicago swept its most hated rivals and biggest nemesis, the Detroit Pistons, in the Eastern Conference finals, Jordan addressed those voices.

"They say I can't lead a team to a winning situation, can't make my teammates better," Jordan said. "I feel I am an all-around player. Winning a world championship will show it."

From the outset, the series was billed as the Michael and Magic Show. It was Jordan chasing his first title vs. Johnson going for a last taste of glory. But Jordan, the better individual talent at that precise moment in time, also had the better

Not until June 12, 1991, did the sports world allow its greatest athlete to receive his just due as a champion

supporting cast.

Still, when Lakers forward Sam Perkins, a college teammate of Jordan's at the University of North Carolina, canned a three-pointer with just 14 ticks remaining in Game 1, and Michael failed to hit an open 18-footer with four seconds left, the Bulls found themselves down a game.

Chicago recovered in Game 2 with a team performance unparalleled in NBA history. Jordan, guard John Paxson, forwards Scottie Pippen and Horace Grant, and center Bill Cartwright shot an amazing 73.4 percent from the floor (47-of-64). Jordan's 15-of-18 performance and Paxson's 8-of-8 showing set the tone in a 107-86 triumph. Taking his challenge directly to Magic, Jordan played point guard for the Bulls, directing the attack and handing out 25 assists in the first two games.

Jordan made up for his Game 1 miss by knocking down a Game 3-tying jumper with 3.4 seconds left in regulation. The Bulls stole that game in overtime, stunned the Great Western Forum

crowd and took a 2-1 lead in the series.

After the Bulls rolled in Game 4, 97-82, Jordan sensed the Lakers were almost finished.

"I can taste it and I can smell it," Jordan said at the time. "Maybe I'm overexcited. I'm anxious to go ahead and win it, but I have to be patient. I've been waiting seven years already."

On June 12, 1991, the wait ended.

Ironically, Scottie Pippen, not Jordan, was the star of Game 5 in Los Angeles. Pippen, who had assumed defensive duties against Johnson earlier in the series, showed his offensive prowess by scoring 32 points in a 43-minute effort. Paxson, Jordan's backcourt running mate for so many years, introduced himself to the nation by hitting five back-breaking shots in the final four minutes. Jordan tallied 30 points and 10 assists, his fourth double double of the series. The final: Chicago 108, L.A. 101. Jordan had his title and finally had found a cure for the Ernie Banks Syndrome.

"It's total satisfaction," Jordan said in the locker room, in between smooches of the world championship trophy. "I always felt I played the style of basketball to win, but a lot of people didn't agree, saying I shot too much, scored too much.

"This is the time I've waited for. It's been a seven-year struggle for me, for the city and for the franchise, too. We started from scratch, we started from the bottom. I never gave up hope that this would happen."

A year later, it would happen again. This time, he would celebrate in front of *his* fans in Chicago. •

Kent McDill covered the 1990-91 NBA Finals for the Daily Herald.

flashDANCE

1991-92 NBA Finals
Bulls 4, Trail Blazers 2

BY MELISSA ISAACSON

There would be no tears this time around. Nor the innocence borne of a first-time champion. Oh, there was joy. Anyone who witnessed Michael Jordan's celebratory jig atop the Chicago Stadium scorers tables that warm June evening certainly can attest to that. But it was a different player who held aloft the Larry O'Brien Trophy from the one a year before. A different man even.

Jordan's basketball achievements were legendary during that 1991-92 season, the Bulls' second consecutive championship drive. He led the league in scoring for the sixth consecutive season with his 30.1-point average, and capped the regular season with his second MVP Award, another berth on the All-Star and All-Defensive teams and a spot on the fabled Dream Team.

Along the way, he missed just two games — both Bulls losses; scored 56 points in the Bulls' decisive Game 3 victory over Miami in the first round of the playoffs; helped clinch the next round with 42 points in Game 7 against New York; then closed out the team's second consecutive Eastern Conference championship with 16 of his 29 points coming in the fourth quarter of Game 6 against Cleveland.

In the Bulls' blowout of Portland in Game 1 of the NBA Finals, Jordan amazed even himself with a surreal, record-setting performance in which he scored 35 first-half points, including six three-pointers. His 46 points paced the Game 5 victory, and his 12 fourth-quarter points in Game 6 helped wrap up the second title and his second straight Finals MVP honor.

But it was as trying a year as Jordan ever had experienced in his 29 years.

"Very few people go through their lifetime without scars," he said at the time. "And I went through a six- or seven-year period without them. Now I've got to mend them and move on."

The scars were deep as the Jordan image absorbed one blow after another. First there was the controversial best-seller (*The Jordan Rules*) that looked beyond the closed doors of the locker room and practice gym to reveal a man so driven by competition that it left him at times looking like anything but the smiling persona in television and magazine ads.

And no sooner had the furor died down than there was an uproar over his whereabouts when the rest of his team visited the White House and scrutiny over his choice of golf companions that ultimately drew a reprimand from the league.

For the first time, fans questioned his appeal, and Jordan wondered if the fame was worth the effort. "From a financial standpoint, it's worth it," he admitted. "But away from that, it has been a burden to a certain extent."

And so here was baggage to lug along while trying to celebrate a second NBA title. As a player, Jordan's goals were simple — prove to the basketball world that the first championship was no fluke. As an icon, however, the answer called for an inner motivation that ironically led him to realize why he loved the game in the first place.

"It has driven me more because all of the distractions have been just that, distractions," he said. "But the cure for that has always been basketball for me. That's my medicine."

And he took it like a sweet spoonful of sugar, immersing himself in the game and not coming up for air until he hopped onto that scorers table, leading his teammates in a giant snake dance that seemed to take all 18,676 people present along with it.

Jordan spoke later of being a bit selfish, of wanting to win this title for himself and his teammates. And reflecting on the past season, he said the turmoil had forced him to grow.

"I think people have gotten a more diverse picture of Michael Jordan, not just from the positive side but some negative stuff and some humanistic stuff, as well," he said. "So, it's taken a lot of the pressure off. Hopefully, we'll all learn something from this year. I know I've learned. I know I've matured."

The words would come back to haunt him the very next year, but then maybe Jordan was prepared for that. "The scars won't go away," he said, "but you know you're going to be a better person because of them."

It would be a long "off"-season, the longest of his career, following his dance at Chicago Stadium. And more scars, along with another special triumph, would make their unmistakable marks on Jordan later that summer in Barcelona, Spain. But that Olympic flame was a mere flicker compared to the red-hot party Jordan would cook up for Dream Team buddy Charles Barkley and the Suns. •

Melissa Isaacson covered the 1991-92 NBA Finals for the Chicago Tribune.

Despite numerous off-court distractions, Michael surprised even himself by taking his level of play even higher

threeFEAT

1992-93 NBA Finals
Bulls 4, Suns 2

BY PAUL LADEWSKI

Michael Jordan and Charles Barkley, both draped in the good ol' red, white and blue (to hide their Reebok labels), stepped off the gold medal platform in Barcelona, Spain, about the same time.

Barkley went his way, winning league MVP honors, posting up Godzilla and singing opera in television commercials, and carrying his new team, the Phoenix Suns, to the promised land.

Jordan went his way, carrying the weight of the world on a pair of shoulders that had been put to the test in recent years. The tribulations started after the Bulls' second title when Jordan refused to break a golfing date to attend a White House reception. Then came the flap about Dream Team warm-up suits and the Olympic Village snub. A much publicized gambling trip to Atlantic City on the eve of a playoff game and a tell-all book by a golfing buddy who claimed Michael was addicted to gambling topped off a troubling year for the game's biggest name. Despite a seventh consecutive scoring title, Jordan felt as if he was living in a nightmare and couldn't wake up.

So when Barkley, who delivered a dream season in his Phoenix debut, and Jordan met with the 1992-93 NBA crown on the line, guess who won?

Jordan in six, of course.

"I kind of put my foot in my mouth before the season," Jordan says of his preseason prediction. "I thought the third time that the pressure would be off. We'd be doing something that we had already done twice, and since no one had won three straight in 25 or 26 years, there wouldn't be as much

pressure as the second one.

"But this was a lot harder than anything I've done in my life in the game of basketball."

Never before has a player endured a tougher beating off the court only to come out No. 1 on it.

"We've gone through a lot this year, and I personally have gone through a lot. To cap it off this way is great," Jordan said after winning. "Now that this team has become part of history, it's a very gratifying feeling for me."

The latest title has prompted the inevitable questions. What inquiring minds mostly want to know is whether the three-peat Bulls deserve to be placed on the same pedestal as Larry Bird's Celtics and Magic Johnson's Lakers, their championship contemporaries.

"We're all sitting here thinking, 'If you took Michael Jordan away from this team . . .',," Magic says. "I mean, you've got a lot of average players. On another team, you may not see the same Scottie Pippen. All the other guys, too."

Magic was right, sort of. Although Pippen continued to excel, the Bulls fell on hard times. The events in June 1993 simply validated Jordan's rank on the short list of all-time greats, perhaps even moved him to the head of the class. What's more, it left no doubt that these Bulls were and continue to be Michael's team.

That the Bulls relied on Jordan like no championship team in sports history was never more apparent than in the decisive Game 6. With a 10-point lead and the hardware staring them in the face, the rest of the Bulls suddenly

experienced cold feet. In fact, the blistering-hot Suns pitched a fourth-quarter shutout until Jordan drained a free throw with 5:51 left to play. By then, Paul Westphal's crew had built a slight lead and was starting to believe they were, as Westphal told the press prior to the game, a team of destiny.

Of course, the game will be remembered best for John Paxson's game-winning three-pointer with four seconds left in regulation. But without Jordan's nine-point run in the final quarter, Chicago's only points before Paxson's bomb, the Bulls would have been heading back to the Windy City for Game 7 to face a team on a serious roll.

Yet Michael, who averaged a playoff-record 41 points in the Finals, was the one talking about destiny.

"It's something we set out to do, and it's something no one can ever take away from us," Jordan exclaimed. "It's something for a team to win three in a row in this era when there is so much talent in the league and so much parity. We feel we should be considered as one of the best teams of all time. Individually, my goal was to win three straight because it was something that Isiah [Thomas] never did, something Magic and Bird never did. It says something to me that I've been able to do that.

"Ten years from now, when my kids are grown, I'll look back on winning three straight and have a proud smile on my face," he concluded. "Now I just want to take a vacation and play a lot of golf."

Fore!   •

Paul Ladewski covered the 1992-93 NBA Finals for the Southtown Economist.

Michael scaled a mountain of controversy to reach a peak no athlete ever may achieve again

Brushes of Brilliance

His incandescent smile, midair maneuvers
on the hardwood and fanciful foray into
baseball have provided inspiration for
a host of artists. Whatever the medium,
Michael Jordan certainly presents an
irresistible subject. Sit back and enjoy
your very own art gallery devoted solely
to the sports world's masterpiece.

Andy Yelenak

Martin Gembecki

Jonathan E. Benash

April Anselona

Bill Waddle

Dan Smith

Richard Larson

Joey Boyack

Eric Franchimon

James Mellett

Vernon Wells

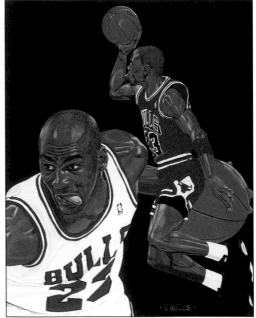

Dan Gardiner

Michael R. Jordan

Chuck Feist

Andy Yelenak

Alan Studt

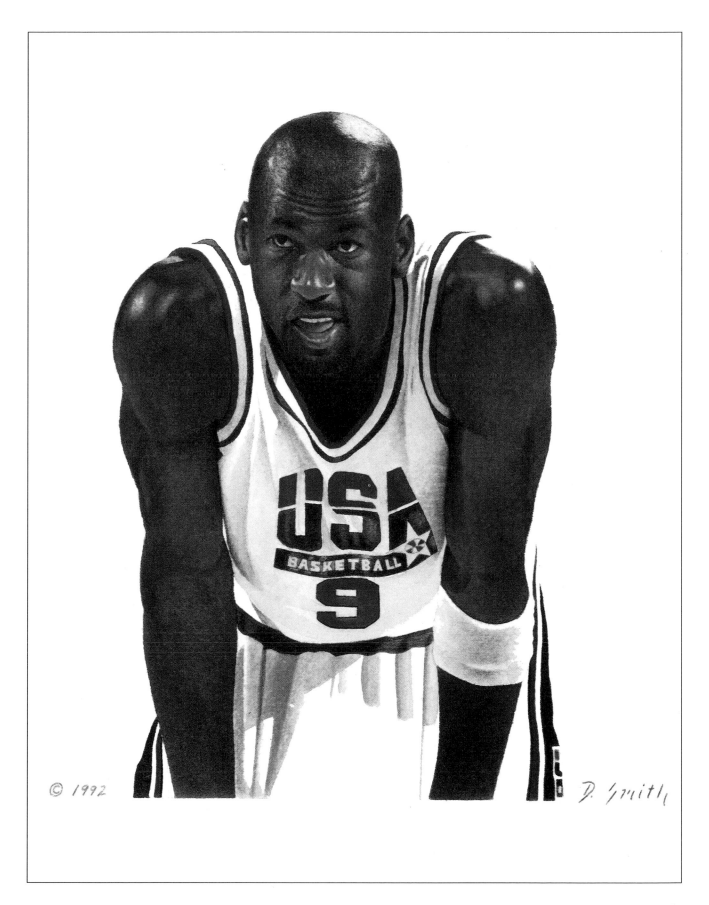

© 1992

D. Smith

Dan Smith

Mike George

Andy Yelenak

Edward Witham

Bull market

Once upon a time, Michael Jordan cards got lost in the shuffle. Today, his picture on a card translates into one of the hobby's most cherished — and valuable — keepsakes.

t here was a time, believe it or not, when collectors couldn't have cared less about basketball cards. Even Michael Jordan cards.

Not so long ago in the mid-1980s, Jordan's two key issues — his 1984-85 Star Extended Rookie Card and his mainstream 1986-87 Fleer RC — could have been purchased in a package deal for around 10 bucks.

Oh, how things have changed.

Today, a deal for those two Jordan issues, assuming the cards are in top condition, will set a collector back

the equivalent of a down payment on a house in the suburbs. They stand easily as the most

PHOTOGRAPHS BY BRAD NEWTON

cherished, not to mention expensive, cards of their time. With a price tag topping $2,000 in top grade, the '84-85 Star Jordan XRC (#101) stands in a class all

alone: No other mainstream card of an active or recently retired athlete in any sport comes near matching its value. And of all of Michael's cards, none has equaled his '86-87 Fleer RC (#57) in popu-

Old Fleer and Star sets remain popular among today's hobbyists, thanks largely to No. 23's appearance.

larity or notoriety. Featuring a photo that captures Jordan in midflight on the way to one of his classic thundering jams, its current

• 56 •
MICHAEL JORDAN

value between $750 and $1,000 in top grade dwarfs all others in that famous 132-card set.

So why have Jordan's cards become so highly regarded? Even before Michael's shocking retirement announcement in October 1993, the demand for his cards was so strong that collectors were willing to shell out hundreds, or even thousands, of dollars for the more desirable Jordan issues.

"Supply and demand, period," explains Willy Erving, a longtime basketball card dealer from the Houston, Texas area. "In most collectors' minds, he's the best player of his generation. No ifs, ands or buts about it."

But talent alone didn't lift His Airness to those immeasurable heights. Jordan also was unquestionably the most popular athlete on the planet. Here in the States, baseball's Nolan Ryan and football's Joe Montana are considered legends in their own right. But put them in Italy, Spain or Israel and you'll have yourself a pair of wealthy tourists. Send Jordan overseas and you get pandemonium.

Jordan's worldwide star power is the result of a carefully designed marketing program that, since 1985, has made him the most recognized and ex-

posed athlete of our time. Jordan's face seems to pop up everywhere. In addition to his status as the world's

23 Michael Jordan, 6-6, Guard

greatest basketball player, one could add world's greatest shoe, cereal and soft drink pitchman to that list without much argument. That overwhelming exposure raised Jordan's name to a level that transcended the game — and also contributed to his decision to walk away at the height of his athletic career.

His enormous popularity continues to have a

Where there's a will to get a Jordan card into a promotion, companies will find a way.

direct impact on Jordan's collectibles. For example, Portland's Clyde Drexler, a player with similar talents to Jordan, has his Rookie Card in the same 1986-87 Fleer set as Jordan. But Clyde's card is valued at a fraction of Michael's card, which is not an indication that Jordan is 10 times the player that Drexler is. In truth, the huge difference in values of the two cards relates directly to Jordan's status as a worldwide hero.

Any hoops prospect

today with the credentials Jordan possessed coming out of college — one-time Player of the Year and gold medal-winning Olympian — would have such a huge following in the hobby that his cards would leave a scorch on every collector's want list. In the mid-'80s, however, basketball cards basically were shunned by hobbyists, most of whom zealously pursued baseball cards.

Before the Boom

The only basketball cards available at the time were printed by the Star Company, a small manufacturer based at that time in Elkins Park, Pa. In addition to Jordan's first card appearance on his '84-85 Star XRC, which was distributed in that season's Bulls team bag, Michael appeared on two other cards in an Olympic/Special bag: one recognizing him as a member of the 1984 Olympic Team and the other honoring his selection as 1985 Rookie of the Year.

Star's unique distribution of its cards through team bags resulted in dealers typically selling them at a retail price of $3 to $7.

"When the Star Company cards came out for 1984-85, nobody wanted them," recalls Steve Gold of

"His return already has increased card sales. I expect it to spark interest in his Rookie Card again. It has been quiet for so long, this should give it a boost. I expect his baseball material to die off the more time goes by. Interest in his new cards that show his return should be great."
JIM REDDEL — Baseball Card Unlimited, Indianapolis, Ind.

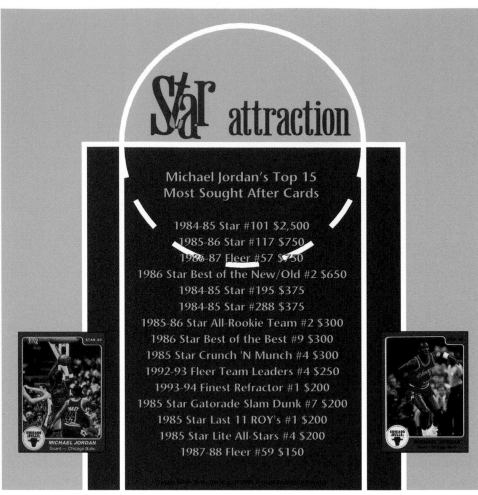

GRAPHS BY AMY BROUGHER / LISA O'NEILL

Star attraction

Michael Jordan's Top 15 Most Sought After Cards

1984-85 Star #101 $2,500
1985-86 Star #117 $750
1986-87 Fleer #57 $750
1986 Star Best of the New/Old #2 $650
1984-85 Star #195 $375
1984-85 Star #288 $375
1985-86 Star All-Rookie Team #2 $300
1986 Star Best of the Best #9 $300
1985 Star Crunch 'N Munch #4 $300
1992-93 Fleer Team Leaders #4 $250
1993-94 Finest Refractor #1 $200
1985 Star Gatorade Slam Dunk #7 $200
1985 Star Last 11 ROY's #1 $200
1985 Star Lite All-Stars #4 $200
1987-88 Fleer #59 $150

AU Sportscards in Skokie, Ill. "We bought 30 to 40 Bulls and Olympic/Special sets and sold only 10 of them in two years. We priced both bags at $7 apiece throughout that entire time period."

Steve Taft, a Southern California dealer who specializes in basketball cards, remembers the days when basketball cards collected more dust than profit. "There was a time," Taft says, "when you could get the entire 1984-85 Star set for $45-$50."

Erving says that initially Star cards weren't accepted by mainstream collectors as legitimate cards. "Many people considered them similar to a Broder or unlicensed issue."

Here's Fleer

When Fleer decided to revive its participation in the basketball hobby with its 132-card set in 1986-87, Jordan was an established superstar lighting up NBA scoreboards wherever he played. In just his third season, Michael averaged a league-leading 37.1 points per game — the first of a string of seven scoring titles, matching Wilt Chamberlain's all-time record.

Unlike Star, Fleer chose to market its cards in wax

packs and boxes on a national level at both retail and hobby outlets. Packs that now sell for $200 or more originally were marked with a suggested retail price of 50 cents. Boxes of 36 packs that now move for a hefty $5,000 to $7,000 price tag originally cost collectors between $15 and $18.

"In 1986, we sold Fleer Jordan Rookie Cards for a dollar apiece and complete sets for $15," Gold recalls. "We bought two cases of 1986-87 Fleer basketball, and they lasted us the entire year."

By 1987-88, Jordan was on his way to a second straight scoring crown and his first intense dose of media exposure — thanks to his Nike Air Jordan shoe campaign. Together they resulted in the first market surge for Michael's cards.

"Even though the Lakers and Celtics were dominating the championships, it was Jordan who got everyone's attention," says Jim Woods, owner of Riley's Sportscards in Salem, Va. "Throughout 1987 and the early part of 1988, dealers bought boxes of 1986-87 Fleer wholesale for $10 to break down for the three Jordan RCs, which they turned around and sold for $5 apiece. None of the other cards in the box were worth more than 50 cents. Jordan was definitely the kicker."

By 1988, the basketball card market was giving every

> "As soon as people heard he was coming back, we started fielding calls for his Rookie Card and baseball cards. His Rookie Card had been languishing for the year and a half he was away from basketball. Now, every Jordan card is moving briskly."
> **NED FISHKIN — a Chicago-based dealer**

Whatever uniform he wears, Michael is a magnet for autograph seekers.

indication that it was headed toward a major boom. Dealers with some foresight started to seek out basketball material, specifically Star bags and '86-87 Fleer.

"The first time I noticed a significant change in the basketball card market was when the Fleer Jordan RC jumped from $10 up to $50 almost overnight early in 1989," Erving says.

In relation to the baseball and football card industry, basketball card print runs were anemic. It's estimated that many Star bags were printed in quantities of 5,000 or less. In addition, the 1986-87 Fleer product had a short run. Ted Taylor, director of hobby relations at Fleer, recalls that "the company didn't have great expectations for that product, thus production was pretty low."

By late 1989, the basketball card market was taking the hobby by storm — with Jordan issues at the tip of that storm. "The boom hit in 1989 when Fleer and Hoops released their sets simultaneously," explains Jeff Prillaman, owner of Cavalier Cards in Charlottesville, Va. "All of a sudden, collectors started to compare Jordan to his contemporaries in other sports. Joe Montana's RC [1981 Topps #216] was valued at $200 at the time and people started to think, 'Hey, this Jordan guy is undervalued.'"

With each passing

month, Jordan's key cards increased in value by leaps and bounds. The boom was on.

King of the Hobby

Many basketball card collectors have come to liken Jordan's '84-85 Star XRC to Mickey Mantle's 1952 Topps #311, in that it represents the ultimate collectible among mainstream cards in the player's sport. In many collections, Jordan's '86-87 Fleer RC holds that esteemed position.

Jordan's 1985-86 Star card (#117) ranks as his second-most valuable mainstream issue, and unlike his

XRC, the card is relatively easy to find well-centered due to higher quality control standards implemented by Star. Still, the four-digit price it currently demands keeps the card on most collectors' fantasy wish lists.

For collectors who can't afford those two hobby icons, a number of other early Jordan cards stand out as some of the more desirable mainstream cards available on the market today.

By the '85-86 season, Star decided the Bulls' superstar was worthy of his own 10-card set. The individual cards, which highlight the various stages of his ca-

reer, have yet to reach three-digit values and for some time were a bargain for a Star Jordan card. For that matter, so are the Jordan issues in the various smaller subsets printed by Star between 1984 and 1986.

"Those are his Hottest cards right now," Taft says of such Jordan issues as 1985 Star Crunch 'n Munch All-Stars (#4), 1985 Star Gatorade Slam Dunk (#7), 1985 Star Rookies of the Year (#1) and 1985 Star Lite All-Stars (#4). At values more likely to fit into a collecting budget, these subset cards also were printed in

Continued on page 64

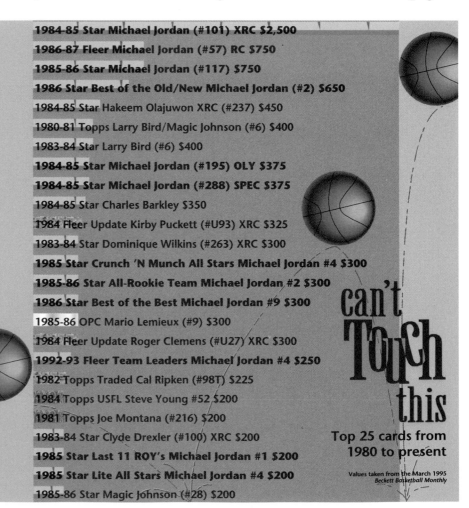

1984-85 Star Michael Jordan (#101) XRC $2,500
1986-87 Fleer Michael Jordan (#57) RC $750
1985-86 Star Michael Jordan (#117) $750
1986 Star Best of the Old/New Michael Jordan (#2) $650
1984-85 Star Hakeem Olajuwon XRC (#237) $450
1980-81 Topps Larry Bird/Magic Johnson (#6) $400
1983-84 Star Larry Bird (#6) $400
1984-85 Star Michael Jordan (#195) OLY $375
1984-85 Star Michael Jordan (#288) SPEC $375
1984-85 Star Charles Barkley $350
1984 Fleer Update Kirby Puckett (#U93) XRC $325
1983-84 Star Dominique Wilkins (#263) XRC $300
1985 Star Crunch 'N Munch All Stars Michael Jordan #4 $300
1985-86 Star All-Rookie Team Michael Jordan #2 $300
1986 Star Best of the Best Michael Jordan #9 $300
1985-86 OPC Mario Lemieux (#9) $300
1984 Fleer Update Roger Clemens (#U27) XRC $300
1992-93 Fleer Team Leaders Michael Jordan #4 $250
1982 Topps Traded Cal Ripken (#98T) $225
1984 Topps USFL Steve Young #52 $200
1981 Topps Joe Montana (#216) $200
1983-84 Star Clyde Drexler (#100) XRC $200
1985 Star Last 11 ROY's Michael Jordan #1 $200
1985 Star Lite All Stars Michael Jordan #4 $200
1985-86 Star Magic Johnson (#28) $200

can't Touch this

Top 25 cards from 1980 to present

Values taken from the March 1995
Beckett Basketball Monthly

Michael Jordan's comprehensive Card checklist

Basketball Cards

- ☐ 1983 Wichita Eagle Star #5 Multiplayer
- ☐ 1984-85 Star #101
- ☐ 1984-85 Star #195 Olympic
- ☐ 1984-85 Star #288 Special
- ☐ 1984-85 Star Court Kings 5 X 7 #26
- ☐ 1985 Bulls Interlake #1
- ☐ 1985 Star Crunch 'n'unch #4
- ☐ 1985 Star Gatorade Slam Dunk #7
- ☐ 1985 Star Lite All Stars #4
- ☐ 1985 Star Last 11 ROY's #1
- ☐ 1985 Star Slam Dunk Supers 5x7 #5
- ☐ 1985 Star Team Supers 5x7 #CB1
- ☐ 1985-86 Star #117
- ☐ 1985-86 Star All Rookie Team #2
- ☐ 1986-87 Fleer #57
- ☐ 1986-87 Fleer Sticker #8
- ☐ 1986 Star Best of the Best #9
- ☐ 1986 Star Best of the New/Old #2
- ☐ 1986 Star Court Kings #18
- ☐ 1986 Star Jordan Set
- ☐ 1987-88 Bulls Entemann's #23
- ☐ 1987-88 Fleer #59
- ☐ 1987-88 Fleer Sticker #2

1986 Star Court Kings #18

- ☐ 1988-89 Bulls Entemann's #23
- ☐ 1988-89 Fleer #17
- ☐ 1988-89 Fleer #120 All Star
- ☐ 1988-89 Fleer Sticker #7
- ☐ 1988 Fournier #22
- ☐ 1988 Fournier Sticker #5
- ☐ 1988 Kenner Starting Lineup #NNO
- ☐ 1988 Panini Spanish Stickers #76
- ☐ 1988 Panini Spanish Stickers #261 All-Star
- ☐ 1988 Panini Spanish Stickers #285
- ☐ 1989-90 Bulls Equal #6
- ☐ 1989 Coke Video #NNO
- ☐ 1989-90 Fleer #21
- ☐ 1989-90 Fleer Sticker #3
- ☐ 1989-90 Hoops #21 All-Star
- ☐ 1989-90 Hoops #200
- ☐ 1989-90 Hoops All-Star Panels #4 Multiplayer
- ☐ 1989 Kenner Starting Lineup One On One #NNO Multiplayer
- ☐ 1989 Magnetables #21
- ☐ 1989 National Sports Daily Promo #1 Multiplayer
- ☐ 1989 North Carolina Coke #'s 13-18
- ☐ 1989 North Carolina Coke #65
- ☐ 1989 Sports Illustrated for Kids Aqua #16
- ☐ 1990 Action Packed Promo* #3
- ☐ 1990-91 Bulls Equal/Star #1
- ☐ 1990 Collegiate Collection Promo * #NC1
- ☐ 1990-91 Fleer #26
- ☐ 1990-91 Fleer All Star #5
- ☐ 1990 Hoops 100 Superstars #12
- ☐ 1990 Hoops Team Night Sheets #4 Multiplayer
- ☐ 1990-91 Hoops #5 All Star
- ☐ 1990-91 Hoops #65
- ☐ 1990-91 Hoops #223A Multiplayer
- ☐ 1990-91 Hoops #358 Team Checklist
- ☐ 1990-91 Hoops #382 Special
- ☐ 1990-91 Hoops #385 Inside Stuff
- ☐ 1990-91 Hoops All-Star Panels #1 Multiplayer

- ☐ 1990-91 Hoops All-Star Panels #2 Multiplayer
- ☐ 1990-91 Hoops CollectAbooks #4
- ☐ 1990 Kenner Starting Lineup #NNO
- ☐ 1990-91 McDonald's Jordan #'s 1-8
- ☐ 1990-91 North Carolina Promos* #NC1
- ☐ 1990-91 North Carolina 200* #3
- ☐ 1990-91 North Carolina 200* #44
- ☐ 1990-91 North Carolina 200* #61
- ☐ 1990-91 North Carolina 200* #89
- ☐ 1990-91 North Carolina 200* #93
- ☐ 1990-91 Panini #91
- ☐ 1990-91 Panini #G
- ☐ 1990-91 Panini #K
- ☐ 1990-91 SkyBox Prototype #41
- ☐ 1990-91 SkyBox #41
- ☐ 1991 Arena Holograms 12th

1988-89 Fleer Sticker #7

National* #3
- ☐ 1991 Cleo Jordan Set
- ☐ 1991 Farley's Fruit Snacks Set
- ☐ 1991-92 Fleer #29
- ☐ 1991-92 Fleer #211 All-Star
- ☐ 1991-92 Fleer #220 League Leader
- ☐ 1991-92 Fleer #375 Team Leader
- ☐ 1991-92 Fleer Pro-Vision #2
- ☐ 1991-92 Fleer Tony's Pizza #33
- ☐ 1991-92 Fleer Wheaties #6 Pro Vision
- ☐ 1991-92 Hoops Prototypes 00 #004
- ☐ 1991 Hoops 100 Superstars #13
- ☐ 1991 Little Basketball Big Leaguers #19
- ☐ 1991 Nike Michael Jordan/ Spike Lee Set
- ☐ 1991-92 Hoops #30

1988-89 Fleer #17

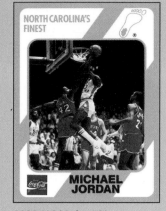

1989 NC/Coke #13

- ☐ 1991-92 Hoops #253 All-Star
- ☐ 1991-92 Hoops #306 League Leader
- ☐ 1991-92 Hoops #317 Milestones
- ☐ 1991-92 Hoops #455 Supreme Court
- ☐ 1991-92 Hoops #536 Active League Leader
- ☐ 1991-92 Hoops #542 Playoffs
- ☐ 1991-92 Hoops #543 Playoffs
- ☐ 1991-92 Hoops #579 USA
- ☐ 1991-92 Hoops All-Star MVP's #9
- ☐ 1991-92 Hoops Slam Dunk #4
- ☐ 1991-92 Hoops Action Photos #11
- ☐ 1991-92 Hoops Action Photos #39
- ☐ 1991-92 Hoops McDonald's #5
- ☐ 1991-92 Hoops McDonald's #55 USA

1989-90 Fleer #21

- ☐ 1991-92 Hoops Team Night Sheet #4A
- ☐ 1991-92 Hoops Team Night Sheet #4B
- ☐ 1991 Kenner Starting Lineup #NNO
- ☐ 1991 Kenner Starting Lineup #NNO
- ☐ 1991-92 Panini #96 All-Star
- ☐ 1991-92 Panini #116
- ☐ 1991-92 Panini #190 All-Star
- ☐ 1991-92 Pro Set Prototypes #0
- ☐ 1991-92 Pro Star Posters* #2
- ☐ 1991 Pro Stars* #6
- ☐ 1991-92 SkyBox #39
- ☐ 1991-92 SkyBox #307 Special
- ☐ 1991-92 SkyBox #333 Multiplayer
- ☐ 1991-92 SkyBox #334
- ☐ 1991-92 SkyBox #408 Game Frames
- ☐ 1991-92 SkyBox #462 Mutliplayer
- ☐ 1991-92 SkyBox #534 USA

- ❏ 1991-92 SkyBox #572 Salutes
- ❏ 1991-92 SkyBox #583 SkyMasters
- ❏ 1991-92 SkyBox Canadian Minis #7
- ❏ 1991-92 SkyBox Minis #534
- ❏ 1991-92 SkyBox Minis #545 Multiplayer
- ❏ 1991 Sports Shots Collector's Books* #1
- ❏ 1991-92 Upper Deck Promos #1
- ❏ 1991-92 Upper Deck #22 Stay in School
- ❏ 1991-92 Upper Deck #34 Classic Confrontation
- ❏ 1991-92 Upper Deck #44
- ❏ 1991-92 Upper Deck #48 Checklist
- ❏ 1991-92 Upper Deck #69 All-Star

1991-92 Hoops #253AS

- ❏ 1991-92 Upper Deck #75 Team Checklist
- ❏ 1991-92 Upper Deck #452 All-Star
- ❏ 1991-92 Upper Deck Award Winner Hologram #1
- ❏ 1991-92 Upper Deck Award Winner Hologram #4
- ❏ 1991-92 Upper Deck Sheet #6 Multiplayer
- ❏ 1991-92 Upper Deck Sheet #14 Multiplayer
- ❏ 1991 Wooden Award Winners #13
- ❏ 1992 ACC Tournament Championship #29 Multiplayer
- ❏ 1992-93 Bulls Dairy Council #3
- ❏ 1992-93 Fleer #32
- ❏ 1992-93 Fleer #238 League Leader
- ❏ 1992-93 Fleer #246 Award Winner
- ❏ 1992-93 Fleer #273 Slam Dunk
- ❏ 1992-93 Fleer All-Stars #6
- ❏ 1992-93 Fleer Team Leader #4
- ❏ 1992-93 Fleer Total D #5
- ❏ 1992-93 Fleer Drake's #7
- ❏ 1992-93 Fleer Team NightSheets #3 Multiplayer
- ❏ 1992-93 Fleer Tony's Pizza #89 Slam Dunk
- ❏ 1992 Hoops 100 Superstars #14
- ❏ 1992-93 Hoops #30
- ❏ 1992-93 Hoops #298 All-Stars
- ❏ 1992-93 Hoops #320 League Leader
- ❏ 1992-93 Hoops #341 USA
- ❏ 1992-93 Hoops #TR1
- ❏ 1992-93 Hoops Supreme Court #SC1
- ❏ 1992 Kenner Starting Lineup #NNO regular
- ❏ 1992 Kenner Starting Lineup #NNO warmup
- ❏ 1992-93 Panini #12
- ❏ 1992-93 Panini #16 Playoffs

- ❏ 1992-93 Panini #17 Playoffs
- ❏ 1992-93 Panini #18 Playoffs
- ❏ 1992-93 Panini #19 Playoffs
- ❏ 1992-93 Panini #20 MVP
- ❏ 1992-93 Panini #102 Fantasy Finals
- ❏ 1992-93 Panini #128
- ❏ 1992 SkyBox USA #'s 37-45
- ❏ 1992 SkyBox USA #105
- ❏ 1992-93 SkyBox #31
- ❏ 1992-93 SkyBox #314 MVP
- ❏ 1992-93 SkyBox Olympic Team #USA11
- ❏ 1992-93 SkyBox School Ties #ST16 Multiplayer
- ❏ 1992 Sports Illustrated for Kids Navy Blue #4
- ❏ 1992-93 Stadium Club #1
- ❏ 1992-93 Stadium Club #210 Members Choice
- ❏ 1992-93 Stadium Club Beam Team #1
- ❏ 1992-93 Topps #3 Highlight
- ❏ 1992-93 Topps #115 All-Star
- ❏ 1992-93 Topps #141
- ❏ 1992-93 Topps #205 50 Points
- ❏ 1992-93 Topps Gold #3 Highlights
- ❏ 1992-93 Topps Gold #115 All Star
- ❏ 1992-93 Topps Gold #141
- ❏ 1992-93 Topps Gold #205 50 Points
- ❏ 1992-93 Topps Archives #52
- ❏ 1992-93 Topps Archives Gold #52
- ❏ 1992-93 Topps Beam Team #3 Mutliplayer
- ❏ 1992-93 Ultra #27
- ❏ 1992-93 Ultra #216 Jam Session
- ❏ 1992-93 Ultra #NNO Multiplayer
- ❏ 1992-93 Ultra Award Winner #1
- ❏ 1992-93 Ultra All-NBA #4
- ❏ 1992-93 Upper Deck #23
- ❏ 1992-93 Upper Deck #62 Multiplayer

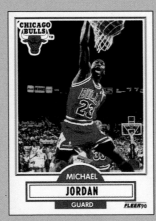

1990-91 Fleer #26

- ❏ 1992-93 Upper Deck #67 MVP
- ❏ 1992-93 Upper Deck #90 Checklist
- ❏ 1992-93 Upper Deck #200 Checklist
- ❏ 1992-93 Upper Deck #310 Checklist
- ❏ 1992-93 Upper Deck #425 All-Star
- ❏ 1992-93 Upper Deck #453 In Your Face A
- ❏ 1992-93 Upper Deck #453 In Your Face B
- ❏ 1992-93 Upper Deck #488 Game Faces
- ❏ 1992-93 Upper Deck #506 Fanimation
- ❏ 1992-93 Upper Deck #SP2
- ❏ 1992-93 Upper Deck 15000 Point Club #PC4

1992-93 Topps Highlight #3

- ❏ 1992-93 Upper Deck All-Division #AD9
- ❏ 1992-93 Upper Deck Award Winner Holograms #AW1
- ❏ 1992-93 Upper Deck Award Winner Holograms #AW9
- ❏ 1992-93 Upper Deck All-NBA #AN1
- ❏ 1992-93 Upper Deck Team MVP #TM1 Checklist
- ❏ 1992-93 Upper Deck Team MVP #TM5
- ❏ 1992-93 Upper Deck Jerry West Selects #JW1
- ❏ 1992-93 Upper Deck Jerry West Selects #JW4
- ❏ 1992-93 Upper Deck Jerry West Selects #JW8
- ❏ 1992-93 Upper Deck Jerry West Selects #JW9
- ❏ 1992-93 Upper Deck European #4 All-Stars
- ❏ 1992-93 Upper Deck European #38
- ❏ 1992-93 Upper Deck European #107 ART
- ❏ 1992-93 Upper Deck European #178 Cards on Collecting
- ❏ 1992-93 Upper Deck European #181 Cards on Collecting
- ❏ 1992-93 Upper Deck European Holograms #2
- ❏ 1992-93 Upper Deck MVP Holograms #4
- ❏ 1992-93 Upper Deck McDonald's #CH4
- ❏ 1992-93 Upper Deck McDonald's #NNO
- ❏ 1992-93 Upper Deck McDonald's #P5
- ❏ 1992-93 Upper Deck Sheets #8 Multiplayer
- ❏ 1993 Fax Pax World of Sport* #7
- ❏ 1993 Fleer #28
- ❏ 1993 Fleer #224 League Leader
- ❏ 1993 Fleer All Stars #5
- ❏ 1993 Fleer Living Legends #4
- ❏ 1993 Fleer NBA Superstars #7
- ❏ 1993 Fleer Sharpshooters #3
- ❏ 1993-94 Finest #1
- ❏ 1993-94 Finest Refractor #1
- ❏ 1993-94 Hoops #28
- ❏ 1993-94 Hoops #257 All-Star
- ❏ 1993-94 Hoops #283 League Leader
- ❏ 1993-94 Hoops #289 League Leader
- ❏ 1993-94 Hoops 5th Anniversary Gold #28

- ❏ 1993-94 Hoops 5th Anniversary Gold #257 All Star
- ❏ 1993-94 Hoops 5th Anniversary Gold #283 League Leaders
- ❏ 1993-94 Hoops 5th Anniversary Gold #289 League Leaders
- ❏ 1993-94 Hoops Face to Face #10 Multiplayer
- ❏ 1993-94 Hoops Supreme Court #SC11
- ❏ 1993-94 Jam Session #33
- ❏ 1993 Nike/Warner Jordan #4
- ❏ 1993 Nike/Warner Jordan #5
- ❏ 1993 Nike/Warner Jordan #7
- ❏ 1993 Nike/Warner Jordan #10
- ❏ 1993-94 SkyBox #14 Playoff Performance
- ❏ 1993-94 SkyBox #45
- ❏ 1993-94 SkyBox Center Stage #CS1
- ❏ 1993-94 SkyBox Dynamic Dunks #D4
- ❏ 1993-94 SkyBox Showdown Series #SS11 Multiplayer
- ❏ 1993-94 SkyBox Promos #1
- ❏ 1993-94 Stadium Club #1 Triple Doubles
- ❏ 1993-94 Stadium Club #169
- ❏ 1993-94 Stadium Club #181 Frequent Flyers
- ❏ 1993-94 Stadium Club 1st Day Issue #1 Triple Doubles
- ❏ 1993-94 Stadium Club 1st Day Issue #169
- ❏ 1993-94 Stadium Club 1stDay Issue #181 Frequent Flyers
- ❏ 1993-94 Stadium Club Beam Team #4
- ❏ 1993-94 Stadium Club Super Team NBA Finals #1 Triple Doubles
- ❏ 1993-94 Stadium Club Super Team NBA Finals #169
- ❏ 1993-94 Stadium Club Super Team NBA Finals #181 Frequent Flyers
- ❏ 1993-94 Third Annual Super Show* #2
- ❏ 1993-94 Topps #23
- ❏ 1993-94 Topps #64 50 Points
- ❏ 1993-94 Topps #101 All Stars
- ❏ 1993-94 Topps #199 Future Playoff MVP
- ❏ 1993-94 Topps #384 Future Scoring Leader
- ❏ 1993-94 Topps Gold #23
- ❏ 1993-94 Topps Gold #64 50 Points
- ❏ 1993-94 Topps Gold #101 All Star
- ❏ 1993-94 Topps Gold #199 Future Playoff MVP

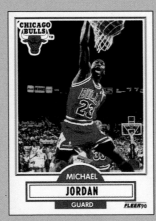

1991-92 Upper Deck #22SiS

- ❏ 1993-94 Topps Gold #384 Future Scoring Leader
- ❏ 1993-94 Ultra #30
- ❏ 1993-94 Ultra All-Defenisve #2
- ❏ 1993-94 Ultra All-NBA #2
- ❏ 1993-94 Ultra All-Rookie Team #2 Multiplayer
- ❏ 1993-94 Ultra Famous Nicknames #7
- ❏ 1993-94 Ultra Inside/Outside #4
- ❏ 1993-94 Ultra Power in the Key #2
- ❏ 1993-94 Ultra Scoring Kings #5
- ❏ 1993 Upper Deck All-Star Weekend #15
- ❏ 1993 Upper Deck French McDonald's #15
- ❏ 1993-94 Upper Deck #23
- ❏ 1993-94 Upper Deck #166 Scoring Leader
- ❏ 1993-94 Upper Deck #171 Scoring Leader
- ❏ 1993-94 Upper Deck #180 Multiplayers

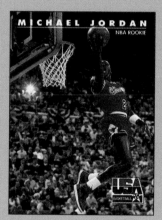

1992-93 SkyBox USA #38

- ❏ 1993-94 Upper Deck #187 Multiplayers
- ❏ 1993-94 Upper Deck #193 Playoffs
- ❏ 1993-94 Upper Deck #198 Finals
- ❏ 1993-94 Upper Deck #201 Finals
- ❏ 1993-94 Upper Deck #204 Finals
- ❏ 1993-94 Upper Deck #213 Multiplayer
- ❏ 1993-94 Upper Deck #237 Signature Moves
- ❏ 1993-94 Upper Deck #438 Breakaway Threat
- ❏ 1993-94 Upper Deck #466 Skylights
- ❏ 1993-94 Upper Deck #SP3
- ❏ 1993-94 Upper Deck All NBA #AN4
- ❏ 1993-94 Upper Deck All NBA #AN15 Checklist
- ❏ 1993-94 Upper Deck Locker Talk #LT1
- ❏ 1993-94 Upper Deck Mr. June #Set
- ❏ 1993-94 Upper Deck Triple Double #TD2
- ❏ 1993-94 Upper Deck Box Bottoms #2
- ❏ 1993-94 Upper Deck European #5 All Star
- ❏ 1993-94 Upper Deck European #33 In Your Face
- ❏ 1993-94 Upper Deck European #43 All-Division
- ❏ 1993-94 Upper Deck European #86 Fanimation

1984-85 Star #101

- ❏ 1993-94 Upper Deck European #90 Fanimation
- ❏ 1993-94 Upper Deck European #118
- ❏ 1993-94 Upper Deck European Award Winner Hologram #1
- ❏ 1993-94 Upper Deck European Award Winner Hologram #9
- ❏ 1993-94 Upper Deck Holojams #H4
- ❏ 1993-94 Upper Deck Pro View #23
- ❏ 1993-94 Upper Deck Pro View #91 3-D Jams
- ❏ 1993-94 Upper Deck SE #JK1
- ❏ 1993-94 Upper Deck SE #MJR1
- ❏ 1993-94 Upper Deck SE Behind the Glass #G11
- ❏ 1993-94 Upper Deck SE USA Trade #5
- ❏ 1993-94 Upper Deck Sheets #1
- ❏ 1994-95 Collector's Choice #23
- ❏ 1994-95 Collector's Choice #204 Profiles
- ❏ 1994-95 Collector's Choice #240
- ❏ 1994-95 Collector's Choice Gold Signature #23
- ❏ 1994-95 Collector's Choice Gold Signature #204 Profiles
- ❏ 1994-95 Collector's Choice Gold Signature #240
- ❏ 1994-95 Collector's Choice Silver Signature #23
- ❏ 1994-95 Collector's Choice Silver Signature #204 Profiles
- ❏ 1994-95 Collector's Choice Silver Signature #240
- ❏ 1994-95 Collector's Choice Blow Ups #23
- ❏ 1994-95 Collector's Choice Blow-Ups Autographed #23
- ❏ 1994-95 Upper Deck Michael Jordan Heroes Set
- ❏ 1994 Upper Deck Launch Tour Sheet*
- ❏ 1994-95 Collector's Choice Spanish #'s 211-219
- ❏ 1994 Upper Deck Nothing But Net #1 Multiplayer
- ❏ 1994 Upper Deck Nothing But Net #5
- ❏ 1994 Upper Deck Nothing But Net #7 Multiplayer
- ❏ 1994 Upper Deck Nothing But Net #9 Multiplayer
- ❏ 1994 Upper Deck Nothing But Net #12 Multiplayer
- ❏ 1994 Upper Deck Nothing But Net #13
- ❏ 1994 Upper Deck Rare Air Set

1991-92 Hoops Playoffs #543

- ❏ 1994-95 Collector's Choice Gold Signature #402 Dr. Basketball
- ❏ 1994-95 Collector's Choice Gold Signature #420 Checklist
- ❏ 1994-95 Collector's Choice Silver Signature #402 Dr. Basketball
- ❏ 1994-95 Collector's Choice Silver Signature #420 Checklist
- ❏ 1994-95 Topps TMB #121

Baseball Cards

- ❏ 1991 Upper Deck #SP1
- ❏ 1994 Action Packed Scouting Report #23
- ❏ 1994 Classic Minor League #1
- ❏ 1994 Collector's Choice #635 Up Close
- ❏ 1994 Collector's Choice Gold Signature #635 Up Close
- ❏ 1994 Collector's Choice Silver Signature #635 Up Close
- ❏ 1994 Collector's Choice #661
- ❏ 1994 Collector's Choice Gold Signature #661
- ❏ 1994 Collector's Choice Silver Signature #661
- ❏ 1994 Fun Pack #170
- ❏ 1994 SP Previews #CR2
- ❏ 1994 SP Holoview Blue #16
- ❏ 1994 SP Holoview Red #16
- ❏ 1994 Sports Illustrated for Kids Blue #270
- ❏ 1994 Ted Williams Gardiner #DG1
- ❏ 1994 Upper Deck Minor League #MJ23 Silver

- ❏ 1994 Upper Deck Jewel Sheet
- ❏ 1994 Upper Deck USA #85
- ❏ 1994 Upper Deck USA Gold Medal #85
- ❏ 1994 Upper Deck USA Jordan's Highlights Set
- ❏ 1994-95 Finest #331
- ❏ 1994-95 Flair #326
- ❏ 1994-95 SkyBox E-Motion #11
- ❏ 1994-95 SkyBox NBA E-Motion N-Tense #N3
- ❏ 1994-95 SP Promo #23
- ❏ 1994-95 SP Tribute Card
- ❏ 1994-95 SP Championship Playoff Heroes #P2
- ❏ 1994-95 SP Championship Series #410
- ❏ 1994-95 Collector's Choice #402 Dr. Basketball
- ❏ 1994-95 Collector's Choice #420 Checklist

1986-87 Fleer #57

- ❏ 1994 Upper Deck Minor League #MJ23 Gold
- ❏ 1994 Upper Deck #19
- ❏ 1994 Upper Deck Electric Diamond #19
- ❏ 1994 Upper Deck Diamond Collection #C2
- ❏ 1994 Upper Deck Next Generation #8
- ❏ 1994 Upper Deck Next Generation Electric Diamond #8
- ❏ 1994 Upper Deck Scouting Report #'s SR1-SR5
- ❏ 1995 Collector's Choice #500
- ❏ 1995 Collector's Choice Gold Signature #500
- ❏ 1995 Collector's Choice Silver Signature #500
- ❏ 1995 Collector's Choice SE #238
- ❏ 1995 Collector's Choice SE Gold Signature #238
- ❏ 1995 Collector's Choice SE Silver Signature #238
- ❏ 1995 Sports Illustrated for Kids Navy Gold/Silver #349
- ❏ 1995 Upper Deck Minor League #45
- ❏ 1995 Upper Deck Minor League Future Stock #45
- ❏ 1995 Upper Deck Minor League Organizational Profiles #OP6
- ❏ 1995 Upper Deck Minor League Jordan Scrapbook Set
- ❏ 1995 Upper Deck #200
- ❏ 1995 Upper Deck Electric Diamond #200
- ❏ 1995 Upper Deck Steal of a Deal #SD15

Racing Cards

- ❏ 1995 Upper Deck #135 Championship Pit Crew
- ❏ 1995 Upper Deck Gold Signatures #135 Championship Pit Crew
- ❏ 1995 Upper Deck Silver Signatures #135 Championship Pit Crew

Soccer Cards

- ❏ 1993 Upper Deck World Cup Honorary Captains* #HC3
- ❏ 1993 Upper Deck World Cup Contenders Honorary Captains* #C3

Denotes multisport set

Through the years, card company editors have discovered it's impossible to produce a boring Jordan card front.

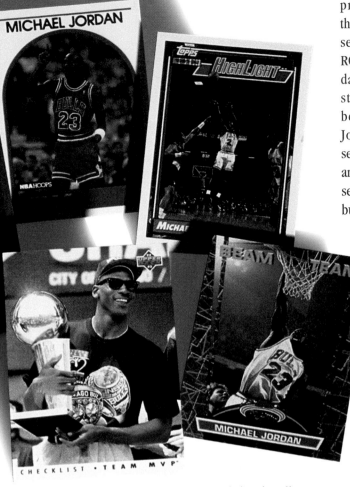

Continued from page 60
runs estimated to be in the same neighborhood as those of Star's regular sets. Recently, the hobby has focused its energy on tracking down the multitudes of Jordan's 1991-93 inserts.

Almost lost in the attention bestowed upon Jordan's '86-87 Fleer RC is his sticker (#8) from that season's Fleer set. Twelve cards and one sticker were inserted into each Fleer wax pack. The complete sticker set is composed of 11 stickers, thus in theory 11 wax packs should yield enough cards (132) and stickers (11) to make a complete set of each. Although the Jordan sticker is just as scarce as his RC, the sticker is worth just a fraction of his Rookie Card's value. This is due mostly to the affinity collectors have

for RCs, plus the lore the Jordan Fleer RC has attained through the years. As tough as regular-issue '86-87 Fleer cards are to find well-centered, the stickers are even more difficult to find without centering problems. Many stickers also have wax stains on the backs.

Jordan's 1989-90 Fleer

card (#21) will set a collector back the price of a decent meal, but landing a Fleer Jordan card from the late '80s is a great addition to any collection.

Budget Relief

Hoops' inaugural set in 1989-90 featured the enormously popular David Robinson RC (#138). The

"He's the greatest player and he's proving it every game. A lot of people are coming in our store for Jordan cards who don't really collect at all. They just want to have a Michael Jordan card."
NACHO ARREDONDO — general manager of San Diego Sports Collectibles

product sold well due to the relentless pack-busting search for more Robinson RCs, resulting in an abundance of singles of superstar cards that suddenly became quite affordable. Jordan's two cards in the set, his regular issue (#200) and All-Star card (#21), will set collectors back just a few bucks each.

During the next two years, the basketball card hobby experienced further growth and witnessed card manufacturers overestimating the surge of collectors focusing on the sport, resulting in a number of heavily printed sets in '90-91 and '91-92. Of course, some good came from the booming growth of the hobby, too: The situation created opportunities for collectors of all ages and incomes to pick up any number of the Jordan cards that were printed.

In 1992-93, basketball card collecting welcomed two new manufacturers into the hobby, as well as a flood of red-Hot rookies into the NBA. While the many RCs and insert issues of newcomers Shaquille O'Neal and Alonzo Mourning dominated the hobby headlines, Michael continued to make his mark. Just ask the lucky collectors who pulled a ***Continued on page 66***

Air mail

Taking aim at Michael's annual two million fan letters, Jackie Banks has her hands full at all times

Jackie Banks works for the most famous ex-athlete in the world — and doesn't even like sports.

Jackie is Michael Jordan's administrative assistant. Her full-time occupation is sorting through Jordan's fan mail, an assignment she's handled for four years and likely will continue, regardless of how many letter openers she wears out.

"It's a nice job, but some people don't understand it's still work," she says. "It's a lot of responsibility. You can't relax, or you'll fall behind."

Letters sent to Jordan through the Chicago Bulls are packaged in boxes and delivered to Banks. She estimates Jordan receives 5,000 letters per week — or, if you prefer, two million letters a year. The volume increases during peak periods, such as after the Bulls win an NBA championship or near Jordan's Feb. 17th birthday.

General fan letters and autograph requests are forwarded to Nike, Jordan's shoe endorsee and also sponsor of his fan club. Nike, in turn, sends back 5-by-7 inch color photos with reproductions of Mike's autograph and a "thanks for writing" letter.

Other, less mainstream requests are handled personally by Banks.

"It's impossible for Michael to accommodate everyone," she says, "but he tries. At the least, I'll send a letter back."

Jordan, of course, is an extremely popular subject of charity fund-raising requests. "By now all the charities are aware of Michael's generosity," Banks explains. "It used to be that as long as the requests were reasonable, were on appropriate stationery to weed out the individuals,

and were sent four to six weeks in advance, they were taken care of. But it's gotten to the point where Michael just has to say no sometimes.

"It's very hard to come up with criteria that determine which charities he helps and which he doesn't, because they're all worthy," Jackie continues. "And they don't understand, because they want 'just one autograph.' He would need to be here 24 hours a day signing autographs to handle them all."

Nonetheless, Michael annually fulfills the requests of more than 400 charities.

Even if a fan's letter isn't on official charity stationery, the chance still remains that Michael will personally read his mail — especially now that he has more free time. Reveals Banks, "He sees a great deal of it. I show him anything out of the ordinary, letters that are touching, business proposals, whatever. He comes by quite often to pick up his mail and keep in touch with his fans."

As hobbyists might expect, Jordan constantly is bombarded with invitations, from little Johnny's birthday party to presidential banquets. "Michael gets invited to everything," Banks acknowledges. "Once he was even invited to a hog-calling contest."

Think that's strange? Try unwrapping some of the countless gifts sent to Jordan.

"Since I've worked here he's received five pairs of wooden shoes . . . from five different people!" Banks says. "I don't get it."

Obviously, the chance of obtaining Jordan's autograph through the mail is slim. But at least collectors know that their letters, and the other 5,000 per week addressed to His Airness, land in good hands. •

BY THEO CHEN

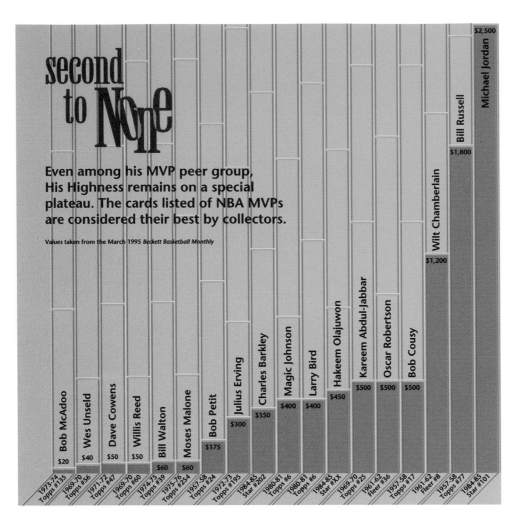

second to None

Even among his MVP peer group, His Highness remains on a special plateau. The cards listed of NBA MVPs are considered their best by collectors.

Values taken from the March 1995 *Beckett Basketball Monthly*

Player	Card	Value
Bob McAdoo	1973-74 Topps #135	$20
Wes Unseld	1969-70 Topps #56	$40
Dave Cowens	1971-72 Topps #47	$50
Willis Reed	1969-70 Topps #60	$50
Bill Walton	1974-75 Topps #39	$60
Moses Malone	1975-76 Topps #254	$60
Bob Petit	1957-58 Topps #24	$175
Julius Erving	1972-73 Topps #195	$300
Charles Barkley	1984-85 Star #202	$350
Magic Johnson	1980-81 Topps #6	$400
Larry Bird	1980-81 Topps #6	$400
Hakeem Olajuwon	1984-85 Star #XX	$450
Kareem Abdul-Jabbar	1969-70 Topps #25	$500
Oscar Robertson	1961-62 Fleer #36	$500
Bob Cousy	1957-58 Topps #17	$500
Wilt Chamberlain	1961-62 Fleer #8	$1,200
Bill Russell	1957-58 Topps #77	$1,800
Michael Jordan	1984-85 Star #101	$2,500

Continued from page 64
1992-93 Stadium Club Beam out of a pack. The 21-card Beam Team set is randomly inserted into Stadium Club Series II packs at a rate no greater than one per 24 packs, thus putting into perspective the difficulty of landing Michael's card.

This year, the attraction for Jordan's new issues continues to be one of the few constants in a hobby that's always changing. As a spokesperson for Upper Deck, Jordan was involved personally with the creative process for the company's '93-94 Michael Jordan's Flight Team set.

Jordan Jewels

To the ultimate Jordan collector, much of the mainstream material is far too commonplace. For those hard-core hobbyists, only the rare, the obscure and the oddball will do for their Jordan collections. There's plenty to choose from, too.

Star Company got the jump on everybody by printing oversized (5-by-7 inches) cards in addition to their standard-sized (2-1/2 by 3-1/2 inches) cards in the mid-'80s. Three of these postcardlike sets include early Jordan cards.

Star's '84-85 Court Kings features Jordan in its second series, while Star's 1985 Slam Dunk Supers set captures Jordan (#5) in midflight — in his vintage black-and-red Air Jordan shoes — en route to a vicious reverse slam. Star's 1985 Team Supers set, of which just 4,000 are believed to have been printed, is a 40-card set showcasing Jordan (#CB1) and his wagging tongue in a classic drive to the hole.

Jordan's shoe and apparel company, Nike, also has produced two sets of cards featuring its main spokesman. In 1985, Nike produced a five-card, multi-sport set of 5-by-7 inch postcards. In 1991, Jordan was the center of attention in a six-card set of standard-sized cards boasting photos from his various ads.

Other oversized Jordan cards that have been produced over the years include his 1985 Bulls Interlake issue (one of two cards sponsored by the Boys Scouts of America) and his various Entenmann's bakery issues. Equal sweetener teamed with the Bulls in 1989-90 to produce an oversized 11-card team set. The next season, Equal joined forces with Star to produce a second regional Bulls team set honoring the Bulls' 25th anniversary.

Most of Jordan's other non-mainstream cards, including such unique 1988

> *"Because of the baseball strike, everyone needed a boost. Jordan gave us that in a huge way. Everything with his name on it is flying. There's been a big jump in baseball cards, too. Everyone wants to have a baseball card of Jordan since they figure he's seen the last of that game."*
> **MIKE BLAIR — Atlanta Sports Cards**

issues as Spanish cards printed by Fournier and Kenner's Starting Line-Up cards, are listed in the current issue of *The Sport Americana Basketball Card Price Guide and Alphabetical Checklist.*

Collectors interested in cards featuring Jordan during his collegiate career at North Carolina finally saw their wishes come true in 1989-90, when Collegiate Collection printed a 200-card set — sponsored by Coca-Cola — honoring legendary coach Dean Smith and Tar Heels stars from the past. Not surprisingly, Jordan wound up featured on seven cards (#'s 13-18 and 65). The next year, the company produced one more set, this time including five Jordan cards (#'s 3, 44, 61, 89 and 93).

Food for Thought

Hungry collectors have satisfied their tastes for cards and food in recent years by finding NBA cards distributed through various food products. And, of course, Jordan frequently is the key player featured in these card promotions.

McDonald's restaurants have joined forces with both Hoops and Upper Deck in recent years to offer cards with their meals. In 1991-92, Hoops created a 70-card set (62 nationally distributed cards plus eight regionally distributed Bulls cards) for McDonald's. Last season, Upper Deck teamed up with McDonald's to distribute a 50-card set available only at the restaurants.

Pizza lovers could land a Jordan card in packages of Tony's Pizzas in either 1991-92 or 1992-93, while collectors who prefer munching on chips

Michael cemented the path for Fleer, Hoops and Upper Deck to make their fast break into the basketball card hobby.

could chase down a mini (1-1/4 by 1-3/4 inches) Jordan 1991-92 SkyBox card in a Hostess/Frito-Lay promotion. Hobbyists who can't pass up desserts could find a Jordan 1992-93 Fleer card (#7) in packages of Drake's cake products.

Meanwhile, Jordan continues to be the featured star in such out of the ordinary sets as Panini's 1991-92 and 1992-93 sticker sets, a 1992-93 Fleer/Shell 12-card sheet honoring the Bulls' first two championships, and

Impel Marketing's 110-card Olympic set honoring the members of the 1992 Dream Team

Hoops and SkyBox also produced Olympic card sets that include the Bulls' super-

star in 1991-92 and 1992-93. And Upper Deck's unique cardlike holograms, which have been produced the last two seasons, honor Jordan for his league-leading scoring and for being selected MVP.

Finally, as a preview of its 1993-94 release, SkyBox

"Jordan really has never slowed down here. During his baseball career it was tough to sell some of his higher priced NBA cards like the Star Company cards. We have people wanting signed basketballs, pictures, etc. I bet we don't have more than three or four cards right now. Once we get things in, they go."
ORVE JOHANSSON — The Baseball Card Company, Largo, Fla.

distributed packs to its registered dealers and select members of the media at the 1993 National Sports Card Collectors Convention in Chicago. Included in the packet was an unnumbered card of you-know-who.

It's rather obvious that attempting to assemble a thorough collection of Jordan cards is like trying to stop Jordan one-on-one — it's the hobby's supreme challenge. Many of Mike's earlier cards are priced beyond the limit of most collectors' budgets, and many of his other cards are incredibly tough to find, requiring years of searching to uncover.

Even in light of Michael's retirement, the allure of obtaining a key Jordan issue will remain strong for many basketball card collectors. His play made him one of the greatest in the game, and his cards turned him into a hobby icon whose issues will stand as the most cherished in collections worldwide for years to come. •

Grant Sandground is pricing coordinator for the Technical Services department of Beckett Publications.

michael Mania

Want to realize a collector's fantasy? Obtain Michael's autograph, find his magazine covers, or — gasp! — retrieve his golf ball.

O n a basketball court, Michael Jordan can do anything he pleases. Off the court, however, he remains trapped. Cornered by his popularity. Imprisoned by his fame.

Everywhere Michael goes, he's recognized — and a frenzy almost always ensues. Activities the general public takes for granted are unthinkable for Jordan. Ever try to watch a movie while a theater full of people asks for your autograph? Such is the price of being the most famous athlete in the world.

At 6-6 and sporting his trademark shaved head,

Michael can't very well blend into crowds. As for previous sports heroes, forget Mickey Mantle — Jordan's worldwide popularity equals the levels once attained by Babe Ruth and Muhammad Ali.

Even when he retired from hoops and became a strikeout victim in the minor leagues, his popularity continued to soar. Now that he's back where he belongs, expect his name to shine even brighter.

Predictably, the immense fame and adulation surrounding Jordan translate

into an incredible, almost insane, level of demand for items associated with him. This applies to items as commonplace as

a Wheaties box or magazine cover to more

Hobbyists hungry for a Jordan collectible that's not captured on his 2-1/2 by 3-1/2 piece of cardboard whetted their appetites on McDonald's Happy Meal prizes.

BY THEO CHEN

treasured memorabilia, such as a game-worn uniform.

Want to know how crazy Michael Mania can get?

Consider the peaceful game of golf, which, as everyone knows, is Jordan's favorite pastime. Although Michael's plans may include an attempt to qualify for the PGA tour, his drives and approach shots occasionally stray off the fairway, even into ponds.

At recent charity golf tournaments whenever a Jordan ball has splashed into a water hazard, fans have dived after it. They may not be as foolish as you think. Jordan's golf balls carry His Airness' monogram, and are treasured additions to any MJ collection.

In the more mainstream market, basketball cards and equipment are two of the more commonly traded types of Jordan items. One strange incident during the middle of the 1989-90 season saw the two normally separate worlds of cards and equipment overlap.

The Bulls were in Orlando to play the Magic during that team's inaugural season.

Before the game began, someone stole Jordan's No. 23 Bulls jersey from the visitor's locker room — forcing Michael to wear a No. 12 jersey during the first half of play. At halftime, the Bulls sent a team representative to the Orlando Arena concourse to purchase a Jordan replica jersey from the Magic-owned sporting goods and souvenir store.

The game-worn jersey business was turned on its ear when No. 23 decided not to play in anymore NBA games.

Jordan then wore the replica jersey for the remainder of the game.

Were it any other Bulls jersey, finding a replacement at a souvenir shop would have been unthinkable. Then again, who would dare enter an NBA locker room to steal the jersey of anyone but Michael?

In a bizarre twist, this incident was documented — then "undocumented" — on cardboard. Sam Vincent's 1990-91 Hoops card #223 originally depicted Jordan underneath the basket wearing the No. 12 jersey. After receiving several queries about the card, Hoops released a replacement Vincent card in Series II that featured a different photo with Michael nowhere to be seen.

Stealing is not the way to obtain game-worn Jordan equipment. But getting his memorabilia through legitimate channels has become harder.

"In the last couple of years, Jordan has become aware of how much his stuff is worth," says Bob Sebring of Sebring Sports in Sevierville, Tenn. "The supply is shrinking. . . . Now he saves most of his stuff for close friends and relatives."

What little "stuff" is out there remains in constant demand.

"He's the No. 1 most-requested athlete for sports memorabilia," Sebring says. "Right now, I have at least 10 people who have him on their want lists and want us to call them first."

Sebring recently sold a game-worn Jordan home jersey for $4,750 and an away version for $3,850. Both jerseys were sold before the ad was published in a hobby publication, and Sebring received "at least 50 calls" once his ad did run.

If you think those prices are a bit steep, check out the going rates for three Jordan jerseys from the Sept. 8, 1993, Richard Wolffers auction. An autographed Jordan 1982 North Carolina road jersey sold for $19,000; an autographed 1984-85 rookie season jersey sold for $15,000; and an unsigned

> *"Jordan stuff definitely has picked up. We've had a lot of demand, not necessarily for the real expensive cards, but for the other cards. There's a lot of cards that go from 50 cents to $5. He's been in the news and that has an impact on what people buy."*
> **KEVIN SAVAGE — Sports Gallery, Sylvania, Ohio**

1992 Olympic Dream Team jersey sold for $21,000.

Had the auction been held after Jordan's retirement, those numbers likely would have skyrocketed even higher.

Picture Perfect

If you've seen enough of Michael on television, you might want to stay away from the newsstand and the grocery store. His face seems to adorn more magazine covers than Madonna, President Clinton and Elvis. And with good reason — Jordan covers sell.

Look no further than the country's leading sports publication, *Sports Illustrated*. Prior to his retirement, Jordan had appeared on the cover 26 times, second only to Ali's 32.

Michael's first cover appearance was the Nov. 28, 1983, college basketball preview issue, when he still wore the powder blue and white of the University of North Carolina Tar Heels. The issue is tough to find, and sells for up to $25 in Mint condition.

Of the plethora of covers showcasing Jordan, perhaps the most notable is No. 19, the Dec. 23, 1991, issue honoring Jordan as Sportsman of the Year and featuring a hologram image of Michael's face on the cover. Despite being less than two years old, copies of that issue in Mint condition with no subscription label currently sell for up to $15. While that magazine was being shipped to subscribers, rumors circulated about copies being stolen from mailboxes and other postal facilities. Heck, even the swimsuit issues don't cause that much of a fuss.

Other recent Jordan *SI*s sell for about cover price, but they're noticeably more difficult to find than other issues.

The number of additional publications boasting Michael's mug on the cover are too numerous to mention. But one particular publication is notable for its uniqueness.

Residents in the Chapel Hill area received a neat surprise in 1982 — a phone book with a special cover showing Jordan hitting the NCAA championship-winning shot. The caption reads, "North Carolina Is *The State Of The Champions*." The item's estimated current market value is $25-$50 — not bad for something that once was free.

Sign of the Times

Even if Jordan had time to catch his breath, there's no way he could answer all his mail. Conceivably, Michael could spend every waking moment of every day signing autographs and still not satisfy the phenomenal demand.

Jordan's fan mail alone long ago required him to hire a full-time, slightly over-worked assistant (*please see related story, page 65*).

In recent years, Jordan — like many megastar celebrities — has understandably cut corners in an

> *"He will restore interest in his lower-dollar material, but I doubt it will have an effect on his Rookie Cards and expensive cards. I think it will have an impact on his baseball cards in a big way. There are so few of them, now there won't be any more. His cards showing him wearing No. 45 already are hot topics."*
> **TOM LOBSIGER — Indianapolis, Ind.**

effort to save time and sign for more people. Depending on the situation and the item, Jordan's signature can vary significantly from the pristine example found on the Wheaties box. A hurried signature on a card, for example, may appear to be little more than an "M" and a "J."

But no matter how sloppy, Michael's autograph on almost anything is in constant demand. Signed Jordan cards, color photos or magazines are easy sells at $30 and often bring as much as $100. Autographed basketballs sell from $125 to $250.

"I sell Jordan stuff real well when I get it," says Richard Moody of Moody's Sports Autographs in Warner Robins, Ga. "Demand for him is steady and strong."

Jordan autographed baseballs are among Moody's top sellers. After Jordan took batting practice with the Chicago White Sox (as depicted on 1991 Upper Deck baseball card #SP1), those autographs took off. After playing in the White Sox's minor league system for a year and a half, Jordan's baseball autographs went through the roof. Now that he's hung up his spikes, who knows how hot signed baseballs will go for.

Through the years, Jordan has made fewer and fewer public appearances, and when he has appeared, he's become increasingly reluctant to sign.

"It's gotten real tough the last couple of months," Moody says. "After they won their third championship, he basically dropped out of sight."

In fact, after the tragic murder of his father, Michael couldn't attend his own charity golf tournament, and he sent his friend Charles Barkley in his place.

Bart Richards, a 16-year-old collector from Salt Lake City, is one of countless autograph hounds who targeted Jordan when the

Finding new ways to use Michael's likeness produced some rather interesting results over the years. But a Michael Jordan thermos might be pushing the limit.

Bulls came to town. In February, 1992, Richards waited in the team hotel lobby, and even chipped in with friends to pay for a night's stay when hotel personnel threatened to kick them out since they didn't have a room key.

The game was scheduled for Monday night. Richards staked out the lobby on Sunday night and Monday. Jordan finally appeared on Monday morning, apparently on the way to a workout. He refused to sign on his way between the room elevator and the parking garage elevator. Richards dashed outside the hotel and down the ramp to the parking garage with his Jordan poster flapping in the wind.

"I asked him for his autograph as soon as he stepped out of the elevator," Richards recalls. "He said, 'Man, you should be in school.' I told him it was a career ladder day, and I didn't have school. Jordan said, 'You don't have that,' and took off."

Although Richards came up empty that time, he did get Jordan to sign on the way into the hotel the next year. Then, at a charity golf

Even though some Jordan figurines barely look like Jordan, they remain popular items.

tournament in Lake Tahoe, Jordan actually recognized him. "He looked at me and said, 'I'm not going to sign for you until you tell me where you're from.' I did, and he signed," Richards says.

Richards, of course, knows that his Jordan autographs are real. As one might expect with a signature holding such demand and value, many fakes probably are being sold as the real thing.

But aside from getting stuck with a fake autograph, it's almost impossible for a hobbyist to go wrong collecting any type of Jordan memorabilia.

Michael still remains the yardstick all other athletes are measured against.

And almost anything that bears Jordan's image will have a luster that will never fade. •

Theo Chen is a Price Guide analyst for Beckett Publications.

dreamSeqU

As ringmaster of the greatest sports show on Earth, Michael won his

Patrick Ewing rips the ball off the glass and outlets to John Stockton, who delivers a perfect bounce pass to Michael Jordan. His Airness ends the play with a one-handed, no-nonsense slam. Quickly turning his focus to defense, Jordan steals the inbound pass and tosses a no-look gem to Charles Barkley, who nearly tears down the backboard as two bewildered defenders run for cover.

And so it went for members of the 1992 Olympic Dream Team, the most talked about sports team in the history of the world.

Losing the men's basketball title in the 1988 Olympics was unacceptable for a country used to dominating the amateur hardwood. Discounting the 1980 boycott, the United States had won every prior men's basketball gold, except for the 1972 debacle in Munich, when the Soviet Union beat the Americans on a last-second, highly disputed shot.

But after John Thompson's team failed even to reach the gold medal game — losing to the Soviets in the semifinals — the U.S. Olympic Committee turned up the heat. Allowing professional superstars to compete for the '92 gold medal guaranteed success.

USA vs Angola	116-48	Gold Medal Game	Quarter Finals:	
USA vs Croatia	103-70	**USA 117**	USA vs Puerto Rico	115-77
USA vs Germany	111-68	**CROATIA 85**	Semi Finals:	
USA vs Brazil	127-83		USA vs Lithuania	127-76
USA vs Spain	122-81			

Draped in the old red, white and blue, Michael and his fellow Dream Teamers wrapped up their summer vacation with a gold medal and a smile. The card back on 1992-93 Barcelona Plastic, a hard-to-find issue in SkyBox Series I, details the Team of the Century's run to glory.

By Steve Richardson

eNCe

...econd Olympic gold and launched his popularity into another universe

Never before — and probably never again — had so much talent appeared on the same team. Jordan, Ewing, Stockton, Barkley, Magic Johnson, Larry Bird, Karl Malone, Scottie Pippen, Chris Mullin, David Robinson and Clyde Drexler represent the best the NBA had to offer. Duke standout Christian Laettner was the token amateur representative.

Thrills and Spills

The Dream Team experience for Jordan was a rollercoaster ride. The peaks were the team's superb play; the valleys were the controversies that he and his teammates faced at every turn.

In one game during the Tournament of Americas in Portland, which the Dream Team won by an average of 51.5 points a game, Jordan actually talked about his golf game on the court with Panama guard Eddie Chavez. Brazil's Marcel de Souza sniped that his team was in Portland to play basketball, not to get a tan and play golf.

"What they worried about is what we do to prepare ourselves to play," said Jordan, who on several occasions played 36 holes of golf on game days during both tournaments. "I play golf because it relaxes me. Once I step on the court, I am going to play, and they are going to get the best out of Michael Jordan."

When the team was being organized, there was speculation that Jordan wouldn't even play. He really didn't want to give up his off-season of golf, anticipating yet another grinding championship run in June. And he already owned a gold medal for his stellar performance in the 1984 Olympics. Why would this time be any different?

But this *was* different. This was a showcase team — the best ever — playing on the world's biggest stage. If Jordan hadn't played, it would have been like owning a Rolls Royce without having any gasoline to get it on the road.

In Barcelona, Jordan did play, but without the flair that had made him the most recognized basketball player on the planet. Jordan wanted to blend in with his fellow Dream Teamers. He wanted to be "just one of the guys."

On the court, he was somewhat successful. On a team that averaged an Olympic record 117.3 points per game, Jordan averaged 14.9 points. Although that ranked him second only to Barkley (18.0), 10 Dream Teamers averaged at least eight points. Jordan also handled point guard duties when Magic was injured. Michael's 4.8 assists a game, fifth best in the Olympics, showed that he was intent on sharing the spotlight. He was stellar on defense, averaging an Olympic-best 4.6 steals a game.

"I'm not going to do anything to take away from this team or try to take away from the rest of these players," Jordan said at the time. "My ego is not that way."

Every now and then, though, Jordan would flash one of his trademark moves just to keep things interesting. "He will show what he can do," Magic says. "Just to remind you."

From the start of training camp in San Diego in late June and all the way through the gold medal game in Barcelona in early August, Jordan was the leader of a traveling show that often resembled a three-ring circus.

Jordan wanted to stay in the shadows. Instead, he got questions like, "How do you feel about the comparisons to God?" from one reporter.

JORDAN'S DREAM TEAM CHECKLIST: 1991-92 Hoops #579, 1991-9

gold RUSH

Every basketball fan in the world is familiar with the Dream Team roster. But how many can name each member of Michael's 1984 Olympic team, the one that outscored its opponents 763-506? Jordan led all scorers with 17.1 ppg. Here's the roster, along with each player's scoring average in the eight-game tournament:

Chris Mullin (11.6)
Patrick Ewing (11.0)
Steve Alford (10.3)
Wayman Tisdale (8.6)
Sam Perkins (8.1)
Alvin Robertson (7.7)
Vern Fleming (7.7)
Leon Wood (5.8)
Joe Kleine (3.3)
Jon Koncak (3.2)
Jeff Turner (1.6)

"Well, actually, I have never seen a god, so I don't know what they act like," Jordan responded. "That's one of the compliments that I don't know how to take, but I will take it and run."

For Jordan and the Dream Team, running was about the only way to escape the fan crunch. From the moment their caravan headed down La Rambla, a busy Barcelona street, to a side street where the tightly secured Hotel Ambassador awaited them, their time belonged to the public.

"They are bigger than the whole Olympics," said Bar-

celona resident David Moss, 15 years old at the time.

"I think I understand why they are not staying in the Olympic Village. For one thing, they would be mobbed," said U.S. volleyball star Steve Timmons.

Every appearance at the Olympic Village caused major autograph scenes. They weren't even off-limits standing with the other athletes at the Opening Ceremonies. For security

Michael displayed flashes of brilliance against the overmatched competition, but for the most part, His Airness decided to keep his feet on the ground and conserve his energy for the '92-93 NBA season.

BRIAN DRAKE

reasons, Jordan wisely was a no-show at this crowded event.

Some perceived Jordan's action as a snub. It was one on a long list of criticisms directed toward Michael and his teammates.

No Contest

They were hassled for not staying in the Olympic Village in Barcelona. They were mocked for their golf games on game days. But when the dust settled and the ball was tipped off, the Dream Team lived up to its advance billing.

And that's saying something.

The United States outscored its opponents by an average margin of 43.8 points. Their closest margin of victory was 32 points. It was like watching the Harlem Globetrotters toy with the Washington Generals.

While the United States was blowing out its opposition, Jordan was in the middle of a full-blown controversy over — of all things — the gold medal ceremony.

Long before the Dream Teamers took care of Croatia, 117-85, to win the gold, fans were more interested in what Michael would be wearing when he stepped onto the winners' platform.

You see, Reebok had provided the team with warm-up suits. Michael, of course, is Nike's main man.

"That's like [the United States Olympic Committee] asking you to leave your dad," Jordan said of wearing the Reebok outfit.

Five other Nike teammates faced similar dilemmas, but Jordan seemed caught alone in the storm. A simple question of apparel on the victory stand nearly soiled the entire event.

A compromise finally was worked out whereby the Nike athletes draped American flags over their shoulders to cover the Reebok label. Still, there's no question the Olympics took some of the spring out of Jordan's step.

Despite winning his seventh straight scoring title and a third straight world championship in '92-93, Michael looked somewhat drained during certain stretches. It's likely fans have seen the last of Jordan wearing a Team USA jersey.

"You will see a team of professionals," Dream Team head coach Chuck Daly says, referring to the next U.S. team for the 1996 Olympics in Atlanta. "But I don't think you will see another team quite like this. This was a majestic team."

The best ever.   •

Steve Richardson covered the 1992 Olympic Dream Team for The Dallas Morning News.

OUT

of this

WOR

By Mike McAllister

**Michael Jordan's immense
success off the court has
made him one of the planet's
most recognizable faces**

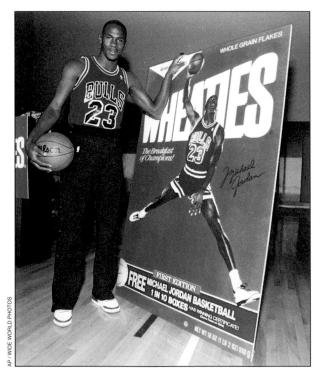

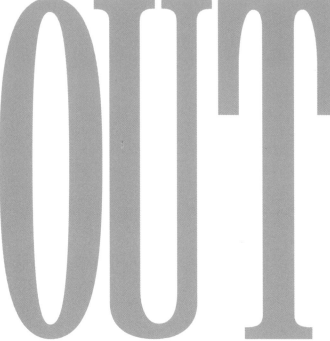

AP / WIDE WORLD PHOTOS

**Michael needs to eat his Wheaties just to keep
up with his hectic commercial schedule.**

He started out simply as Michael Jordan.

Then he became Air Jordan.

Then he teamed with Bugs Bunny to become Hare Jordan.

Now he's Everywhere Jordan.

Thanks to his seemingly endless stream of product endorsements, Jordan the Marketing Giant earned many more millions of dollars than Jordan the Basketball Superstar.

In its most recent list of top product endorsers, *Sports Marketing Letter* listed Michael No. 1 for the fifth con-

heroes such as golfer Greg Norman and rugby star Allen Langer.

Not since heavyweight champion Muhammad Ali has there been an athlete who carried more global appeal.

At the 1992 Summer Olympics in Barcelona, in which the U.S. Basketball Dream Team dominated much of the headlines, Jordan was asked by a reporter how it felt to be God. Many attending the press conference snickered, but there might be some bizarre truth in the question. After all, when it comes to pushing products and watching sales soar, Jordan certainly has no Earthly equal. Everybody wants to wear his shoes, drink his drink, eat his burgers, drive his cars and play his games.

Who's the only character who could upstage Bugs Bunny? Michael, of course.

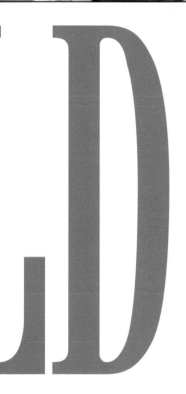

secutive year. He earned $28 million in endorsements, about five times more than his annual salary from the Chicago Bulls. Golfing legend Arnold Palmer was a distant second with $11 million.

Not even his sudden retirement slowed down the master of the air and airwaves.

Through Jordan's commercials, his popularity has long since grown past the boundaries of the sports world. In the United States, he's ranked by one poll as the second most recognizable celebrity behind Bill Cosby. In China, a recent survey of school children listed Jordan and Chinese premier Zhou Enlai as the greatest men in history. In Australia, Jordan received more votes in a popularity poll than homegrown sports

Everything Michael touches, it seems, turns to gold.

"A word like 'superstar' is inadequate," says Brian Murphy, editor of *Sports Marketing Letter*, a monthly trade newsletter.

"Michael Jordan is the quintessential spokesperson," says Patti Sinopoli, group manager of Gatorade communications/public relations.

But why is Jordan so much better as a pitchman than the countless other superstars who have passed through their own eras and left nary a mark in the commercial world?

Sure, Super Bowl quarterback Joe Namath had his day in the sun with those outlandish panty hose ads in the '70s. And yes, Cy Young pitcher Jim Palmer stripped for some memorable underwear commercials in the '80s. And who will forget Olympic gold medalist Mary Lou Retton somersaulting onto America's television screens for Wheaties? But through the years, no one ever has approached the Bulls' world-renowned No. 23.

It's Definitely the Shoes

It all started, of course, with Michael's extraordinary basketball talents. Jordan's remarkable hangtime, his eye-popping scoring totals, his championship rings and his unmatched combination of grace and power made him the sports world's marquee name. No player in any sport dominates a game the way Michael dominates basketball. In fact, no one even comes close. That alone makes Jordan special.

Jordan's winning smile and playful attitude simply adds to his appeal with kids, which in turn, inspires goodwill in parents.

"It's his continued peak of being a championship athlete and his appeal to all ages," says Kathryn Newton, public relations manager for General Mills, the maker of Wheaties. "He's a very good role model for young kids and he's involved in several charitable activities. And yet, adults really like him because of his charisma and poise. Compare him to Larry Bird, who is a very outstanding athlete. The thing Larry didn't have was that kind of charisma that appeals to Americans."

Larry also peaked too soon. Jordan reached his playing zenith at the same time the league's popularity took off.

Before Bird and Magic Johnson entered the scene in '79, the NBA's image was tarnished with little television exposure and a reputation for being soft on players with drug problems. When Jordan left the University of North

SHOE-IN.

Everyone knows Michael wore Air Jordans. How many know he helped design them?

At Nike's
state-of-the-art corporate headquarters in Beaverton, Ore., a suburb of Portland, many of the company's buildings are named after the famous sports figures who endorse its products.

There's the Bo Jackson Building, which houses the company's sports and fitness center. There's the Nolan Ryan Building, which contains the retail and human resources departments. The John McEnroe Building is marketing, and the Joe Paterno Building is the child care center.

But the Michael Jordan Building — like the athlete it's named for — is the most important in Nike's grand scheme. It contains the department that keeps Nike ahead of its competitors and steaming full speed toward the future — research and development.

How appropriate, considering Jordan is the first athlete, according to Nike, to have a shoe mass-produced specifically according to his needs. The revolutionary and immensely popular Air Jordan shoe epitomized Nike's cut-

TIM DeFRISCO/ALLSPORT USA

Step by step, Michael helped win the shoe wars for Nike.

ting-edge technology when it was introduced in 1985.

Just as Jordan put the Chicago Bulls atop the NBA world, the Air Jordan put Nike atop the far more competitive and cutthroat shoe world. The shoe is one of Nike's top sellers.

"The Jordan shoe is the ultimate in performance costume design, made for someone who is constantly playing on center stage," says Mark Parker, vice president of Nike's design and development group.

The marriage of Nike and Jordan wasn't the first between a shoe company and an athlete. During the '50s and '60s, many NBA stars wore Converse's canvas sneakers with Chuck Taylor's signature on the side. And when Larry Bird and Magic Johnson entered the NBA in 1979, ready to turn around a league then struggling for popularity, Converse was there again. The company signed both players to endorsement contracts and "Cons" quickly became the shoe of choice.

But it wasn't until Nike signed Jordan, when Michael turned pro in 1984, that one company and one player combined for a total commitment to one shoe. As with everything else he has done in basketball, Jordan launched the shoe industry into orbit.

"I think even Magic and Larry would agree that Michael has taken the game to a new level," Nike spokesman Dusty Kidd says.

"The Air Jordan shoe was the perfect technology for a player who could jump out of the sky. It implies a feeling of weightlessness. The shoe has a personality. When you think of it, you think of Jordan," Kidd adds. "In fact, if you ask people around the world what 'Air Jordan' is, some will say it's the basketball player. Others will say it's the shoe. The two are synonymous — and you can't say that about another player and his shoe."

Jordan took an immediate interest in his shoe line, meeting with Nike designers to provide input regarding the needs of basketball players. He still flies to Beaverton once or twice a year, and Nike designers travel to Jordan's Chicago-area home at various times to obtain his opinion of new designs.

"There may not be any athlete who has worked as closely with a company to make his shoe as Michael has with Nike," Kidd says.

Will any player ever match the success Jordan and Nike have had with the Air Jordan shoe? Doubtful.

Sure, the contenders are plentiful. Shaquille O'Neal's endorsement of Reeboks and Larry Johnson's deal with Converse ("Grandmama") are two emerging heavyweights. Even at Nike, sales of Air Force shoes endorsed by Charles Barkley skyrocketed during the 1992-93 season when Sir Charles took Phoenix to the NBA Finals.

But no player attracted the attention of the shoe-buying public like Jordan. For example, once when Jordan was pictured in a Chicago newspaper practicing in a prototype Air Jordan shoe, more than 300 requests were made at Chicago's Nike superstore for the shoe — one that hadn't yet been released.

"I don't think anyone will ever recreate the formula Nike has with Jordan," Kidd comments. "Maybe, if someone such as a Dr. J [Julius Erving] comes along. But there are so many different brands out there today that you've got to worry about the dilution factor.

"There have been just a few athletes who have created a special attraction, players such as Babe Ruth or Joe Louis, Muhammad Ali or the Mantle-Maris duo," Kidd says. "We're experiencing the Michael Jordan era."

Now that Michael has returned to the hardwood, all eyes in the shoe business again will be focused on the most famous feet in the world.   •

— *Mike McAllister*

Carolina after his junior season in 1984, his timing couldn't have been better. He caught the NBA's popularity wave — started by Bird and Magic — and has ridden it ever since.

"Several things converged to help make Michael the marketing phenomenon he is today," says Dusty Kidd, a public relations manager at Nike. "No. 1 is Michael the person. Not only is he a great athlete, but he really takes pride in everything he does. No. 2 is Michael off the court. He has personality, style, a sense of honesty — all of those things. No. 3 was the NBA starting to rise again. You ask the demographics of any group what their favorite sport to watch is, and the majority say it's pro basketball. And No. 4 was the product Michael represented. For the first time, it was a product that really reflected the style and needs of a player. Michael can be as innovative as any player, and the shoes he wore reflected that."

Jordan joined the Nike camp in 1984 and helped turn that company into the industry giant.

The image Nike created for Jordan was just as important to Michael's off-court success, though.

In years past when an athlete was used for commercial purposes, what usually transpired was a variation of the "I'm [insert famous athlete's name here] and I like the product so you should, too." Rarely was the man behind the stats showcased.

But Nike and the Portland-based advertising agency of Wieden and Kennedy — with the prodding of Jordan's agent, David Falk — transformed Jordan into much more than just another jock pitchman. Remember the Mars Blackmon "It's Gotta Be the Shoes" spots with Spike Lee? Or Michael's commercials with Bugs Bunny as a teammate? Those weren't commercials, they were events. For the MTV generation, an audience in love with sound bites, the Nike approach with Michael was a winner.

"Nike came up with a whole new way of advertising endorsements," Murphy says. "In the early '80s and before, it was nickel and dime deals. Companies didn't market shoes aggressively. If they did, it was tried and true advertising, like a few clips of a guy playing. 'Joe Blow plays best in XYZ shoes.' Not very effective.

"Nike realized they had the player of the century and asked how they could use the guy to break open the shoe category as a major growth. They invested in Jordan's image. Wieden and Kennedy used film technology such as quick-cut editing and creative footage, not canned footage."

The results for Nike? In each of the past two years with Jordan as pitchman, the company sold nearly 100 million pairs of shoes, which equals about 200 pairs of shoes sold every minute.

With that kind of selling power, it's no wonder the shoe king had Michael's back when No. 23 hung it up.

"Michael Jordan didn't retire from Nike," said Nike chief executive Phillip Knight at the time. "Our nine-year creative collaboration has always been more than an endorsement deal. It is a partnership that will continue, and we have already discussed future plans."

Likewise, Wheaties, who signed Jordan as its national spokesman in 1988, continued its relationship with Michael, as did Gatorade, who made the "Be Like Mike" song a Top 40 hit.

In fact, Jordan's "early" retirement actually may have given him and the products he pitches more credibility.

"It is very seldom that an athlete goes out on top," explains Steve Baker, a sports lawyer who's based in San Francisco. "If he is truly done, if he has

NIKE card SETS

This five-card set issued in 1985 features Nike spokesmen in special set-up shots. The cards were shrink-wrapped and distributed at shoe stores with a Nike purchase. When the set first hit the street, Dwight Gooden, not Michael Jordan, was the key card. Today, the Jordan card sells for about $35 in Mint condition. The other three cards in the set are Lance Parrish, John McEnroe and James Lofton.

This black-and-white Nike card set featuring Michael and fellow pitchman Mars Blackmon (a.k.a. Spike Lee) was issued in a six-card boxed set in 1991. The complete set is listed at $5 in *Basketball Card Price Guide No. 4* by Dr. James Beckett.

1 Earth/Mars 1988
2 High Flying 1989
3 Do You Know 1990
4 Stay in School 1991
5 Genie (Little Richard) 1991
6 Michael Jordan Flight School

truly left, that's very marketable. He is so singularly recognizable."

With so many products to endorse, one question remains: Is Mike oversaturated?

"I don't believe having so many endorsements is a conflict," Newton of

thoughts. "We think he could be less exposed and it wouldn't be too bad," Kidd says. "But the key thing for us is he doesn't strap on a pair of hot dogs or a bottle of Gatorade when he plays. But he does have on our shoes."

Falk says he and his client are extremely particu-

Still, Michael sometimes wondered if Everywhere Jordan had gone so far as to overshadow his real talents — playing basketball.

"Nike has done such a job of promoting me that I've turned into a dream," Jordan said recently. "In some ways, it's taken me away from the game

AP / WIDE WORLD PHOTOS

The day Michael announced his retirement, he became "Bear" Jordan on the New York Stock Exchange. Each of the products he endorses dropped at least 1/8 of a point.

One of Michael's key selling points is that fans know he really uses — or in this case consumes — the products he endorses.

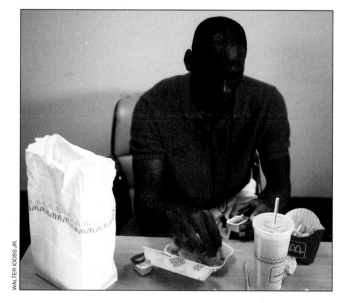

WALTER IOOSS JR.

General Mills replies. "He does the very best job for your product, and he's able to devote the kind of time required for his commitment."

When to Say When

It may seem to viewers that Jordan pops up on their screen every 30 seconds. In fact, the King of Hardcourts declines more offers than he accepts.

"Even though people think Michael endorses everything in the world, he really is selective in what he endorses," adds Sinopoli of Gatorade.

"Certainly, we don't feel he's overexposed. We had the opportunity to establish a relationship with the best athlete around, one we think is particularly appropriate for a product like Gatorade."

But Nike officials have different

lar about what products Jordan is associated with.

"We turn down millions of dollars in commercial opportunities in order to control Michael's name and image," Falk says. "You must make a superstar like Michael scarce enough to be interesting, yet available enough to be popular. It is a constant balancing act, and you must have control to do that."

Yet the Jordan image has become so popular and his following so huge that he no longer can control some events. Jordan's ties with Nike created a 1992 Dream Team controversy when he was forced to wear another company's apparel during the gold medal ceremony. He solved the crisis by draping himself in an American flag, as did fellow Nike pitchman Charles Barkley.

and turned me into an entertainer. To a lot of people, I'm just a person who stars in commercials."

Will there ever be another athlete who matches Jordan's popularity and penchant for peddling product? Perhaps.

Orlando Magic center Shaquille O'Neal certainly has gotten off on the right foot — and the left one — for Nike's top competitor, Reebok.

"Sooner or later, somebody else will come along and match the popularity," Murphy predicts. "It might happen in 1998. Or it might not be until 2038."

But for now, Jordan remains the star attraction.   •

Mike McAllister is an associate editor at Beckett Publications.

By Bruce Martin

Michael Jordan's college career tipped off with a bang, but he quickly learned that playing for Dean Smith's Tar Heels meant no one player comes before the team

When fans reflect on Michael Jordan's career at the University of North Carolina, one game, one moment immediately springs to mind.

The Shot.

Jordan forever will be etched in North Carolina basketball lore for hitting "The Shot" that won an NCAA title for the Tar Heels on March 29, 1982.

"That is the beginning of my career, all the way around," Jordan says of his game-winning 17-footer with 17 seconds remaining against Georgetown in front of more than 61,000 at the Superdome in New Orleans. "That shot gave me more confidence to improve as a player more than any other situation. It gave me the confidence that I could compete on a national level with the competition I had to face."

Jordan's shot didn't clinch the game. Georgetown had plenty of time to set up for a winning basket. But when Hoyas guard Fred Brown mistakenly passed the ball to UNC forward James Worthy, the game was sealed and Jordan, a freshman at the time, became a national star. *(For more on The Shot please see "Nothing but Net" on page 84.)*

"That season, I didn't have to deal with the pressure," Jordan remembers. "That's the difference with that situation and what I had to deal with with the Chicago Bulls.

"When I came into the North Carolina situation, the pressure wasn't on me, it was on James Worthy and Sam Perkins and those guys who had come from the Final Four the year before."

The season before Jordan arrived in Chapel Hill, the Tar Heels had advanced to the NCAA championship game against Indiana, losing a 13-point decision at The Spectrum in Philadelphia. When 1982 tipped off, and with the addition of a skinny kid wearing No. 23, UNC was ranked No. 1.

"After hitting The Shot to win the title in 1982, along with the other accomplishments throughout my college career, it really didn't leave me much to achieve except to duplicate it," Jordan says. "That helped me make my decision to leave school. But at the same time, it gave me the confidence because I didn't really have the notoriety as a big-time player coming into college."

It's difficult to imagine today, but when Jordan signed his letter of intent to play for North Carolina, he was just another basketball player trying to make his mark. "I was wet behind the ears, just happy to be there, and I ended up with The Shot," he says.

Jordan's college career may have started in spectacular fashion, but many felt it never really reached the level it could have. He displayed flashes of brilliance — the occasional no-look pass or highlight film dunk — but many of Jordan's natural abilities were inhibited by UNC head coach Dean Smith and his strict, team-oriented system.

The 1981-82 North Carolina Tar Heels were far from a one-man team. The team that defeated Georgetown, 63-62, to finish the season at 32-2 and give Smith the first of his two NCAA titles was one of the most talented in college basketball history. It included junior forward James Worthy and sophomore center Sam Perkins, both of whom have enjoyed long

Continued on page 85

By Leonard Laye

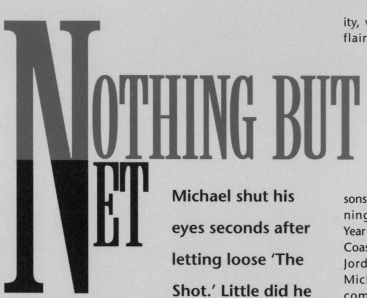

NOTHING BUT NET

Michael shut his eyes seconds after letting loose 'The Shot.' Little did he know that the whole world would open up to him after it swished through.

James Jordan squirmed toward the edge of his seat in the Louisiana Superdome and snapped his eyes shut.

On the arena floor his teenage son, Michael, did the same thing as the ball spun from the tips of his fingers toward the basket. College basketball's national championship hung in the balance.

By the time father and son opened their eyes, the ball had finished a fateful flight through the net and into the lore of the NCAA Final Four. And in that instant, Michael Jordan's life and the face of his sport were changed forever.

It was late evening on March 29, 1982, long before the days of Air Jordan — the high-flying hotshot who never misses when the game's on the line.

This was his introduction to the big time, and all the pressure that comes with it. Jordan's shot, a 17-foot jumper from the left wing with 17 ticks remaining, marked the first time Michael stood in the spotlight and delivered.

Coming into this game of games, there was little reason to believe Michael would be the difference in downing Georgetown, 63-62.

At the time Jordan, 19, was a wiry, almost skinny kid from the North Carolina coastal town of Wilmington, a college freshman with an extraordinary amount of basketball promise. But he was simply another in a long line of super talents wearing the Carolina Blue.

With his leaping ability, wagging tongue and flair for the dramatic, Michael already had experienced a milestone season of sorts, becoming just the fourth freshman to start his first game in Dean Smith's 21 seasons as head coach. Winning the Rookie of the Year Award in the Atlantic Coast Conference proved Jordan was worthy. Yet Michael was still just a complementary player on a balanced, veteran team powered primarily by forward James Worthy and center Sam Perkins, two other NBA stars-in-waiting.

Jordan reached the final game with solid statistics, averaging 13.5 points, 4.4 rebounds and shooting 53.4 percent from the field. His scoring average was just two points below Worthy's, one below Perkins'. Late that season, however, when every player should be hitting his peak, Jordan was mired in a shooting slump.

At halftime of the title game, with UNC trailing by a point, Jordan had four points.

"I'd never been that nervous in my life," Jordan remembers. "My hands were shaking. I couldn't get myself calmed down."

The team's halftime talk helped. Michael's concentration improved, as did his game. Jordan scored six of the Tar Heels' first eight points of the second half. After his early outburst, the scoring responsibilities shifted back to Worthy and Perkins, who kept UNC close. Michael reappeared in a flash for a breathtaking driving layup over Georgetown's shot-blocking phenom Patrick Ewing with 3:26 to play.

The Hoyas slipped in front, 62-61, with 32 seconds remaining. During a timeout, Smith diagramed history.

"We thought Georgetown would be in a zone," Smith recalls. "We came into this game thinking we could throw the lob against their zone, but they were very conscious of it and covered it well."

Smith called a play that would leave Jordan open on the wing if the Hoyas collapsed low on Worthy and Perkins.

"When I heard Coach Smith call my name, I was a little surprised," Jordan admits. "But I didn't want to feel nervous. I just wanted to hit that shot."

The ball went to point guard Jimmy Black on the right wing. He swung it around to forward Matt Doherty, who immediately looked inside for Worthy. As the defense frantically shifted in the paint, Doherty threw the ball back to Black. Black

The Superdome scoreboard flashes the significance of this historic moment.

then threw the ball over the zone to Michael, who was wide open on the left wing.

Jordan jumped, his mouth popping wide open and his tongue flicking out as the ball left his hands. It was a moment he'd dreamed about just hours before, on the team's bus ride from a French Quarter hotel to the Superdome. But now, like his father, he couldn't look.

"I didn't want to watch it," James, now deceased, said at the time.

The world did, and The Shot became a symbol of the Jordan magic, the first of countless game-winning baskets.

"I could never do it again," Michael said in the locker room after the game. "It's frightening to think of how things would have been if I had missed."

He didn't. •

Leonard Laye covered the 1982 NCAA national championship game for the Charlotte Observer.

and outstanding careers in the NBA.

"The intensity just seemed to explode at the right time," Worthy recalls of the '82 title game. "It was almost like a miracle for it to happen that way. It was like a book — an ending to a book."

For Jordan, it was the opening chapter in a basketball career that would launch him on the path to stardom.

Change of Heart

Growing up in Wilmington, N.C., such lofty goals never existed. At least, not on the hardwood.

"I wasn't in tune with professional basketball that much. I was more into the baseball scene," Jordan admits. "The Hank Aarons and the Willie Mays' were the guys I was thinking about when I was a kid. Basketball didn't become much of a focus to me until I started playing and excelling at it later in my years. I really didn't know much about Wilt [Chamberlain] when I was growing up."

Even when Michael fell in love with basketball, he was about as far from a UNC hoops fan as possible.

"I hated [UNC point guard] Phil Ford when I was a kid," Jordan says. "I was a David Thompson fan. Since I went to the University of North Carolina, I understand Phil Ford a lot better now. But at the same time, when I was growing up I really hated him because of his success, his image and his team.

"I was an N.C. State fan."

If Michael hadn't gotten his act together in high school, he would've been lucky just to buy a ticket for the annual N.C. State vs. UNC showdowns. He didn't take basketball seriously in his first two high school seasons, and even was cut from the Emsley A. Laney High team in Wilmington his sophomore year.

"[Being cut] made me more serious about sports," Jordan admits. "Up to that point, I was involved in sports because it kept me out of trouble. It was a hobby. But when I got cut, the humiliation that I got from that situation was really embarrassing. It lit a fire under me to prove to this guy, 'What are you doing? You're cutting me. You're not supposed to cut me.'

"I came back and proved to [my coach] that I was much better than he expected. I got a taste of success and the next thing you know, I wanted more. I started working harder academically as well as athletically and the next thing you know, it all rolled into a ball that has kept rolling up to this point."

Jordan became one of North Carolina's most sought after high school players and finally signed for Smith, who knew Michael's diverse talents would mix well with Worthy and Perkins. Jordan was a starter from the first game of his freshman season, something of which just three other Tar Heels

By Bill Woodward

GROWTH SPURT

Cut from his high school varsity team as a sophomore, Michael soon showed that he was a cut above everyone else

Ron Coley didn't discover Michael Jordan. But he might be one of the first to recognize Jordan's greatness.

"I was driving the van with the cheerleaders and got to the game early, in time to watch some of the JV game," remembers Coley, an assistant coach at Laney High School in Wilmington, N.C. "I saw one of our guys playing as if we were down by a point with 30 seconds left. I looked up on the clock and there were three minutes left and we were down by 20.

"I knew we had something."

The determination that would carry Jordan to the top of his profession already was there. But the amazing athletic ability just was beginning to develop.

The seeds were planted in the Jordan backyard. Michael grew up in a middle-class neighborhood in Wilmington, a town in southeastern North Carolina. The basketball hoop in the Jordan yard was a magnet for the kids in the neighborhood.

Michael's older brother, Larry, was 5-7 and could dunk the ball with both hands.

"Larry used to get the best of Michael, until Mike grew to 6-4," Coley says.

As a sophomore, Michael was of average size — an inch below 6 feet. He possessed a lot of raw talent, but missed making the varsity as a 10th grader. It came down to Jordan and a 6-7 sophomore named Leroy Smith.

Coley believes being cut was a blessing in disguise for young Jordan.

"Michael was the key player of the JV squad. He had 45 points in one game and 47 in another," Coley says. "And he grew a lot that year."

Jordan sprouted to 6-4, and was a starter for varsity head coach Clifton "Pop" Herring as a junior. Fred Lynch, then a Laney assistant who now is the head coach, recalls that first varsity season as one when Jordan began to exhibit his high-flying antics.

"He was beginning to develop into a great player," Lynch says. "He could take over a game when he wanted to."

Jordan was an All-Conference player as a junior on a Laney team that went 13-10.

As a senior, Jordan became a complete package.

can boast. He averaged 13.5 points in 34 games. But regardless of his early success, Jordan quickly learned this was Dean Smith's team.

At UNC, seniors are treated with respect and privileges, whether they're a star or a bench warmer. Conversely, no matter how many high school press clippings a freshman comes to campus with, he is nothing more than a commoner.

"Carrying the balls and the film projector, that is the type of thing that keeps you humble," Jordan says of his freshman chores. "I think that is a key for the young players who come in with all the media attention and hype. It puts them back on the level where they have to build their credibility and respect back to this level.

"I think it was something a lot of us learned from. Everybody has been through it who has played under Dean Smith. You can't think of any great player from North Carolina who didn't go through it."

Learning the Dean Smith way of playing basketball also was a major adjustment for Jordan.

"The practices and everything are so precise," Jordan says. "It's the system, and coach Smith sticks to the system, and no one is above the system. That is a proven fact.

"The system at the University of North Carolina still stands. That catapulted my dream

Dan Dakich did something in college that no one could do in the NBA: He shut down Michael Jordan.

UPI / BETTMANN

He could shoot outside, drive inside and greatly improved his ball-handling skills.

"Pop [Herring] made a great move before Michael's senior season," Coley explains. "We saw all kinds of combination defenses on him when he was a junior — double-teams, triple-teams.

"To solve the problem of how to get him the ball, we let Michael bring it up court."

Jordan poured in nearly 30 points a game and created countless opportunities for his teammates. His incredible leaping ability also became a hot topic.

"There was one game at New Bern [a city about 80 miles northeast of Wilmington], where a player was really dogging Michael all the way up the court, sticking right on him," Coley says. "Then about a step or two past the foul line, Michael just

The Wilmington Buccaneers had a pretty fair go-to guy in No. 23. He's the one with his mouth open.

jumped right over him and slammed one."

Jordan was selected to the All-State team his senior year and barely missed out on Player of the Year honors — an award that went to a flashy scorer from the mountains of North Carolina named Buzz Peterson, who would become Jordan's college roommate and close friend.

"Michael was one of the best kept secrets in the country," Coley says. "He was blessed by God with that body. But I've never seen a more competitive individual. He worked harder than anybody out there, even though he had enough talent that he probably didn't have to."

Winning it all as a college freshman took some

WILMINGTON STAR NEWS

of the sting out of fouling out in a conference semifinal loss his senior year in high school. But the fire he stoked during those high

school years was only a spark compared to what was to follow. •

Bill Woodward is a freelance writer in Garner, N.C.

and career tremendously and it has done that for the other players who were on that championship team."

Regardless of how well-oiled the machine, a championship team must have the heart of a lion. Jordan brought that intangible with him every time he stepped onto the court.

"It would bug him if he lost a drill for a day and had to run after practice," Smith says of Jordan's will to win. "He was so competitive. He may have been the most competitive player I ever had. I've never seen such a competitive spirit. It would kill him to lose a simple drill."

Jordan's competitive spirit pushed the Tar Heels to the pinnacle of college basketball from 1982 to 1984. His sophomore season, Jordan averaged 20 points a game — the highest scoring average of his collegiate career. He was a consensus All-American in 1983 and 1984 and made the All-Atlantic Coast Conference first team both seasons.

But Jordan never returned to college basketball's brightest stage. In 1982-83, the Tar Heels were eliminated by North Carolina State in the ACC tournament semifinals. Later that month, UNC lost to Georgia, 82-77, in the NCAA East Regional championship game.

In 1983-84, the Tar Heels won their first 21 games and threatened to become the first collegiate team to go undefeated since the 1976 Indiana Hoosiers went 32-0. Arkansas ended UNC's regular season streak, and Duke knocked the Heels out of the ACC tourney.

Despite the loss, UNC appeared primed to make a run at the NCAA title, easily defeating Temple in its first tournament game, 77-66. That set up a battle against Indiana in the East Regional semifinals at The Omni in Atlanta. On paper, it should have been a cake walk for the Tar Heels. However, Bobby Knight doesn't coach his Hoosiers with paper.

Somehow, Knight fired up unheralded Dan Dakich to turn in a once-in-a-lifetime performance guarding Jordan.

MICHAEL JORDAN'S UNIVERSITY OF NORTH CAROLINA STATISTICS													
Years	G	FGM-FGA	Pct.	FTM-FTA	Pct.	Reb.	Avg.	Ast.	TO	Stl.	PF-D	Pts.	Avg.
1981-82	34	191-358	53.4	78-108	72.2	149	4.4	61	57	41	91-1	460	13.5
1982-83	36	282-527	53.5	123-167	73.7	197	5.5	55	76	78	110-4	721	20.0
1983-84	31	247-448	55.1	113-145	77.9	163	5.3	64	67	50	70-2	607	19.6
Career	101	720-1,333	54.0	314-420	74.8	509	5.1	180	200	169	271-7	1,788	17.7

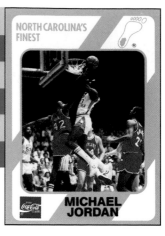

Michael drew two first-half fouls, forcing Smith to sit his main man while Indiana, behind the shooting of freshman Steve Alford, built a comfortable lead. The Tar Heels fought back, but fell four points short (72-68) and were eliminated. Before fouling out, Dakich held Jordan to just nine points. No defender ever held Michael to less than 10 points again.

Knight Moves

That loss marked the end of Jordan's collegiate career. But he had one more journey to make before he entered the NBA. He was a co-captain on the 1984 U.S. Olympic basketball team coached by Knight, which also featured sharpshooter Alford. The team practiced in Bloomington, Ind., that summer, and Knight made certain Michael was well motivated by the time the squad reached Los Angeles.

"The first person I saw when I arrived for practice every day was Dan Dakich," Jordan says, shaking his head.

Jordan also made quite an impression on Knight. The talkative, often controversial coach was asked after the Olympics who was the best college player in the country.

"Michael Jordan — this year, last year, 10 years ago, 15 years ago and at least that far into the future," Knight answered. "I had no idea he was that good of a player until I had him for the 1984 Olympics.

"The kid is a superior athlete — the best I've ever seen."

Smith saw only one logical step for Michael following his glowing performance in the '84 Games.

"Coach Smith gives you some options as a ballplayer," Jordan explains. "He gives everybody an option. He says, 'Your level of skill is at a point where you can go up to another level. We don't push you to go that way, but you have a strong possibility of going in the first five picks of the NBA draft. If you choose to do that, the university will back your decision.'

"If I had stayed another year, I don't think I would have been a better pro," Jordan adds. "I believe, same as coach Smith, that I was ready to step up to another level. It was tough to find something to challenge me day-in and day-out. Most teams were playing me in a diamond-and-one defense,

Sponsored by Coca-Cola, 1989-90 Collegiate Collection printed a 200-card set featuring some of the more famous products of the University of North Carolina. Of course, Jordan's issues (#'s 13-18 and 65) are the highlight. Again in 1990-91 North Carolina 200, Michael's cards (#'s 3, 44, 61, 89 and 93) key the set.

diamond-and-two or box-and-one. All the different defenses I had to face weren't really fun on the collegiate level.

"I had achieved everything possible on the college level, and it was time for me to go and move on to bigger dreams and bigger goals, because I had achieved everything possible."

Smith knew Jordan was going to be a special pro talent, but even this coaching wizard was amazed at the impact Michael had in the NBA.

"His charisma is something I cannot believe," Smith says. "I have never followed Michael Jackson, but if it's anything like Michael Jordan, it must be something.

"When I was out in Los Angeles in 1987 for the North Carolina-UCLA alumni game, I saw a lot of that in Michael Jordan," Smith continues. "We had to get the cops to come and get us out of there because we couldn't get through the crowd of people wanting to see Michael and touch him. He has definitely captured the imagination of fans everywhere."

Despite his immense success in the pay-for-play league, Jordan still reserves a special place for UNC.

"My practice stuff is all Carolina Blue," Jordan says as he pulls out an old pair of basketball shorts that have been used so often the UNC logo has worn away. "It's something I cherish. It's home. It keeps me sane."

Michael also wore a pair of UNC practice shorts under his Chicago Bulls game shorts. Since he hit The Shot more than a decade ago, those colors have served him well. •

Bruce Martin is a freelance writer in Huntersville, N.C.

Michael retains many habits from his Carolina days, including wearing his blue practice shorts under his Bulls uniform.

MICHAEL JORDAN: A Zone All His Own

Only His Shadow Knows
"Michael takes off, hangs in the air until everyone else comes down, and then decides which spectacular shot he'll perform," explains Magic Johnson. "No one on the planet ever has done it better."

"MICHAEL JORDAN'S PLAYGROUND"

In Your Face

The last opponent to hold Michael to less than 10 points in a game was Indiana's Dan Dakich in the 1984 NCAA East Regional final. In the pros, defenders tried everything short of nuclear weapons to ground His Airness.

Lights, Camera, Michael

Maybe Michael would have been better suited to play in Los Angeles. The way he charms a movie camera (like he's doing on his 1992-93 Hoops #382) is worthy of Academy Award attention.

A Diamond in the Rough

Under the watchful eye of Mr. October (Hall of Fame slugger Reggie Jackson, in the background), Michael steps into a pitch at the 1993 Celebrity All-Star Game home run hitting contest at Oriole Park at Camden Yards. As a youngster, Michael fired two no-hitters and dreamed of someday playing big-league ball. Then he sprouted 4-1/2 inches in less than a year. Ironically, Jordan's retirement plan first became known during a baseball game — Game 1 of the American League Championship Series at Comiskey Park. Jordan threw out the first pitch.

Reflections of Greatness

If the NBA could clone Michael, it would do so in a second. "He's been our finest ambassador and greatest player for so long it's tough to imagine the game without him," NBA Commissioner David Stern said during the 1992-93 NBA Finals.

Nice Putt, Mr. Palmer

Michael said he felt more pressure before his round of golf with legend Arnold Palmer than he does when shooting a game-deciding free throw in the NBA Finals. Maybe that's because on the links, Jordan has been known to miss a shot on occasion.

Easy Does It

Out of respect for his foreign opponents, Michael kept his eyes open during the Olympic tournament in Barcelona. But neither Jordan nor his Dream Teammates lost much sleep in claiming the gold medal with an average victory margin of 43.8 points.

Three-Peat

Michael actually appears on card #'s 544 and 545 as 1991-92 SkyBox gave collectors a three-panel look (the other card is #546) at the greatest team in sports history.

Shooter's Touch

A career 85 percent free-throw shooter in the NBA, Michael refined this often overlooked facet of the game into an art form.

Smooth Operator

Michael first shaved his head between his sophomore and junior years in college. "I was disappointed with my sophomore season and I wanted a new start. Shaving my head was part of that," he says. It must have worked. Jordan's bald head became as much a part of the NBA as his trademark baggy shorts, wagging tongue and wristband.

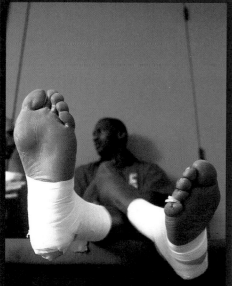

Tremendous Feats

Believe it or not, there aren't tightly wound springs or rocket jets built into Jordan's feet. They're just like everyone else's.

One of a Kind

Appropriately, Jordan's opponents in this computer-enhanced photo (1992-93 Upper Deck Team MVP #TM5) seem to be caught in a time warp. When Michael glided to the hoop, he was in a dimension all his own.

MICHAEL JORDAN • TEAM MVP™

Family Ties

Michael's special bond with his parents, James and Deloris, helped him achieve greatness in the NBA and eventually helped him decide to leave the game at the age of 30.

ANDREW D. BERNSTEIN / NBA PHOTOS

JONATHAN DANIEL / ALLSPORT USA

Etched in Stone

Few will argue with the sentiment chiseled into the base of the statue of Jordan outside the United Center.

Hang Time

In a nationally televised extravaganza last November, the Bulls raised Michael's No. 23 to the United Center rafters — a fitting place considering the amount of time it spent airborne with him in it.

NATHANIEL S. BUTLER / NBA PHOTCS

10 More Years?

Following Michael's retirement, Upper Deck honored his 10 years in the league with a 10-card Heroes insert set in 1994-95 Series I packs. Are we now witnessing the beginning of a second decade of dominance?

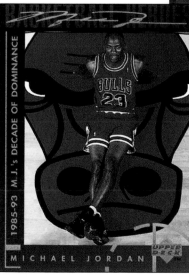

Back for More

The number may be new, but it didn't take long for Michael to show that it's the same old Jordan inside the new uniform.

Flight

No need to search the sky for vapor trails. These cards track the trajectory of Michael's high-flying career.

From the moment his game-winning jumper beat Georgetown in the 1982 NCAA title game, Michael Jordan seemed destined for a soaring basketball career. He left North Carolina after his junior year as a two-time All-American, then starred for the gold medal-winning U.S. Olympic basketball team in 1984. Averaging 28.2 points per game, he ran away with Rookie of the Year honors his first season in the NBA. Two seasons later, he won the first of his seven scoring titles. In 1988, he was selected All-Star Game MVP, named NBA Defensive Player of the Year and won the first of his three league MVP awards. When critics began questioning his ability to lead his team to a championship, he directed the Bulls on a run of three straight titles, climaxed by a 41 points-per-game average in the 1993 Finals against Phoenix.

Pattern

Michael's unique and indelible imprint on the NBA earned him worldwide fame and recognition. His participation on the Dream Team in the 1992 Olympics in Barcelona, where he was greeted as a combination rock star/sovereign king/living deity, merely confirmed his status as a figure of global proportions. The unquestioned favorite subject of the card industry, Michael was as apt to appear on cardboard with filmmaker Spike Lee as soaring with a soccer ball in connection with the 1994 World Cup. When Michael pursued a career in baseball subsequent to retiring from basketball, his popularity merely expanded into another arena. His improbable quest was chronicled exhaustively, and though he ultimately fell short of his baseball goal, the significance of his journey was that it led him to a new beginning in basketball.

New York discovered a stark reality in Michael's fifth game back when Jordan scorched them for 55 points.

UNSTOPPABLE

Michael Jordan continually proves there's no defensive scheme he can't destroy and no defensive wizard he can't embarrass

By Mike Kahn

Preventing Michael Jordan from scoring in a game would have been tantamount to keeping Eric Clapton away from his guitar or keeping Barbra Streisand from singing.

Short of physical damage, it couldn't be done.

Just ask Phoenix Suns head coach Paul Westphal, who tried everything from tough guy Dan Majerle to jitterbug Kevin Johnson against No. 23 in the 1992-93 NBA Finals.

Jordan, the owner of a record-tying seven NBA scoring titles, still was the difference in leading the Bulls over the Suns. En route to his third straight NBA Finals MVP Award, Jordan averaged — yes, averaged — 41.0 points in the six-game series.

"Nobody can guard that guy," Westphal said right after the six-game series. "Sometimes, we made him work hard. Sometimes, he just inflicted his will on us. But stop him? No way."

Theories on how to stop this 6-6 scoring machine began the day he arrived in the NBA in 1984. No answers ever were found. Through nine spectacular seasons, Jordan left a wasteland of defensive schemes in his wake.

He burst into the NBA a year early out of the University of North Carolina. Prior to being named 1984-85 NBA Rookie of the Year, he led the United States to a gold medal in the 1984 Olympics. Vern Fleming, now with the Indiana Pacers, guarded Jordan — or at least tried to — every day in practice on that Olympic team.

"Back then, he just jumped over you," Fleming remembers. "You'd go up to challenge his shot, and maybe somebody else would go up with you, but just as you start to come down, he's still going up. That's what amazed me about Michael then. Nobody really expected him to be as good as he is."

Westphal knew exactly what to expect from Jordan when the Suns squared off against the Bulls last season. Still, answers were at a minimum.

"We were thinking of trying to bring [North Carolina head coach] Dean Smith in," Westphal says. "They say he was the only one ever to stop him."

Of course, Westphal was just kidding, noting that Jordan averaged a "paltry" 17.7 points per game in college. The only time he was close to that mere mortal scoring figure in the pros was in his second season with the Bulls when he broke a bone in his foot, played in just 18 games and averaged 22.7 points.

"He has created this monster of an image on the floor and he had to keep it up," Magic Johnson says. "Besides his incredible talent, there's his pride. That's just as important, maybe more."

Bulls management noticed that part of Jordan's game from his first day with the team. Before Michael arrived in the Windy City, Bulls basketball tended to be a physical game that attacted hard-nosed, low-on-talent, do-anything-it-takes players such as Jerry Sloan, now the Utah Jazz head coach. Jordan mixes incredible talent with an unrelenting will to win.

"I never thought

I would ever see anyone with a bigger heart than Jerry Sloan," Bulls president Jerry Krause says. "But Michael has it. We had poor Pete Myers play against Michael [in practice] for half a season. We found out we can't have young players guard Michael in practice."

No one could guard Michael.

When asked who did the best job on him, Jordan's pragmatism and ego are hard-pressed. "Really, I can't think of anybody," Jordan ponders. "Not really. Well, I guess Dumars."

Detroit Pistons off-guard Joe Dumars, a perennial All-Defensive selection, deserves some sort of prize. Maybe a medal of valor. He's three inches shorter than Michael, not nearly as quick and can't share the same

flight path. Yet, this ordinary Joe gets the nod from Jordan. Dumars' secret: Never let up.

"Nobody can really play him," says Dumars, whose Pistons eliminated Michael and Company in three consecutive playoff series before the Bulls broke the streak in 1990-91. "The only way to do it is to stay with him and keep a hand in his face. Then you just hope the ball doesn't go in. What else can you do?"

Prayer never hurt.

Best Defense: A Good Offense

Early in Jordan's career, when coaches around the league still thought they were dealing with just another great player, there were those who

believed they'd actually solved the problem.

Since Jordan's numbers were lower against the Dallas Mavericks and Washington Bullets, the theory was that Mavericks shooting guard Rolando Blackman, also 6-6, and Bullets gunner Jeff Malone, 6-4, tired out Michael by making him sweat on the defensive end.

Those teams were particularly adept at running him into countless screens, bumping him constantly and overworking him on defense.

Dumars and his stout Pistons teammates became renowned for their relative success against him in the playoffs. Even Jordan would tire under the basketball vernacular of body-punching.

"I knew I had to get stronger," Jordan says. "Everybody was getting a lot more physical with me each year. I couldn't have improved if I didn't figure out how to take it."

Jordan fought back by bulking up. He headed for the weight room and turned his slim 195-pound body into a chiseled 210-pound weapon. And despite the heavier frame, Michael became faster.

Once thought of as a one-dimensional scoring machine in the George Gervin mold, Jordan quickly became a defensive standout. The '92-93 season marked the sixth straight season Jordan was named to the NBA's All-Defensive team. He led the league in steals — many of which he turned into highlight film dunks — three times. And just to top it off, Michael expanded his shooting range each season, while still managing to hit at least 50 percent of his shots. That way, he wasn't wearing himself out driving to the hole on each possession.

"He did things nobody else can

BRIAN SPURLOCK

Defensive wizard Joe Dumars knew he had his hands full when Michael stepped onto the court.

COMPLETE PACKAGE

(Michael Jordan's NBA Regular Season Statistics through 1993)

Yr./Team	G	Min	FGM-FGA	Pct	FTM-FTA	Pct	Off-Def-Tot	Avg	Ast	Stl	Blk	Pts	Avg
'84-85/Chi.	82	3,144	837-1,625	.515	630-746	.845	167-367-534.	6.5	481	196	69	2,313	28.2
'85-86/Chi.	18	451	150-328	.457	105-125	.840	23-41-64.	3.6	53	37	21	408	22.7
'86-87/Chi.	82	3,281	1,098-2,279	.482	833-972	.857	166-264-430.	5.2	377	236	125	3,041	37.1
'87-88/Chi.	82	3,311	1,069-1,998	.535	723-860	.841	139-310-449.	5.5	485	259	131	2,868	35.0
'88-89/Chi.	81	3,255	966-1,795	.538	674-793	.850	149-503-652.	8.0	650	234	65	2,633	32.5
'89-90/Chi.	82	3,197	1,034-1,964	.526	593-699	.848	143-422-565.	6.9	519	227	54	2,753	33.6
'90-91/Chi.	82	3,034	990-1,837	.539	571-671	.851	118-374-492.	6.0	453	223	83	2,580	31.5
'91-92/Chi.	80	3,102	943-1,818	.519	491-590	.832	91-420-511.	6.4	489	182	75	2,404	30.1
'92-93/Chi.	78	3,067	992-2,003	.495	476-569	.837	135-387-522.	6.7	428	221	61	2,541	32.6
TOTALS	667	25,842	8,079-15,647	.516	5,096-6,025	.846	1,131-3,088-4,219.	6.1	3,935	1,815	684	21,541	32.3

do," Magic says. "You could try to force the ball out of his hands, but he's so quick and so strong, he could beat two players. If you challenged him, he'd only come at you that much harder."

The lowly 1992-93 Bullets and up-start shooting guard LaBradford Smith found that out. Smith poured in a career-high 37 points against Jordan on March 19, and he was feeling pretty good about himself after the game despite the Bulls' victory in Chicago Stadium. What he forgot was this was a back-to-back scheduling quirk and the Bulls were coming to the Capital Centre the next night. Jordan promised to ring up 37 in the first half, only to miss a free throw and have just 36 at intermission. Needless to say, he proved his point.

"If someone gets the best of me, I try not to let that happen again," Jordan said after humbling young Mr. Smith. "I try to turn the tables on them."

The Cleveland Cavaliers know all about having tables turned over on them. Twice Jordan eliminated the Cavs with shots at the buzzer.

In 1989, his clinching Game 5 jumper over Craig Ehlo from the top of the key stole the series from Cleveland.

"I thought I had great position on him," Ehlo recalls. "There's no way to stop a shot like that. He just stays in the air and has that touch. There was nothing else I could do."

The Cavs thought they'd found an antidote in the summer of 1992 by signing free agent Gerald Wilkins, designated the "Jordan-stopper" since he'd experienced some success against Jordan while with the Knicks.

Little did they know, there was no cure.

Jordan tore through Cleveland in a four-game sweep of the Eastern Conference semifinals, including 43 points in Game 1 and an 18-footer at the buzzer to end the series. "So much for the Jordan-stopper," Michael chuckled. "They thought they had their problem solved."

Wilkins, who had been a bit mouthy before the series, relented. "Hey, nobody can stop him one-on-one," he said. "All you can do is try to keep good position on him and try to keep him from getting good looks."

But Jordan always got good looks. And his shots always looked good. He was going to get his 30 points a night no matter who was guarding him. But on some special nights, when everything was clicking, Jordan turned in some trademark performance:

• On April 20, 1986, Jordan topped Elgin Baylor's single-game playoff points mark with 63 vs. Boston.

• A year later (April 16, 1987), Michael again rewrote NBA history, establishing an NBA record by scoring 23 consecutive points against the Atlanta Hawks.

• Michael scored a career-high 69 points in a 117-113 overtime victory against the Cavs on March 28, 1990.

• In probably his most awesome offensive display, MJ nailed six three-pointers and scored 35 first-half points in Game 1 of the 1992 NBA Finals against the Portland Trail Blazers. Jordan's reaction after his sixth three-pointer swished through the net: A shrug to Magic, who was part of the NBC broadcast crew sitting in awe on the sidelines. "The rim was like a huge basket and everything was going in," Jordan later said. "I surprised myself at times tonight."

The generally cocky John Starks, considered one of the top defensive

Tough enough to handle when he's earthbound, Michael is a frightening sight to opponents once he takes flight.

HIS TIME

(Michael Jordan's NBA Playoff Statistics)

Yr/Team	G	Min.	FGM-FGA	Pct.	FTM-FTA	Pct.	Off-Def-Tot	Avg	Ast	Stl	Blk	Pts	Avg
'84-85/Chi.	4	171	34-78	.436	48-58	.828	7-16-23	5.8	34	11	4	117	29.3
'85-86/Chi.	3	135	48-95	.505	34-39	.872	5-14-19	6.3	17	7	4	131	43.7
'86-87/Chi.	3	128	35-84	.417	35-39	.897	7-14-21	7.0	18	6	7	107	35.7
'87-88/Chi.	10	427	138-260	.530	86-99	.868	23-48-71	7.1	47	24	12	363	36.3
'88-89/Chi.	17	718	199-390	.510	183-229	.799	26-93-119	7.0	130	42	13	591	34.8
'89-90/Chi.	16	674	219-426	.514	133-159	.836	24-91-115	7.2	109	45	14	587	36.7
'90-91/Chi.	17	689	197-376	.524	125-148	.845	18-90-108	6.4	142	40	23	529	31.1
'91-92/Chi.	22	920	290-581	.499	162-189	.857	37-100-137	6.2	127	44	16	759	34.5
'92-93/Chi.	19	783	251-528	.475	136-169	.805	32-96-128	6.7	114	39	17	666	35.1
TOTALS	111	4,645	1,411-2,818	.501	942-1,129	.834	179-562-741	6.6	738	258	110	3,850	34.7

guards in the NBA, earned respect by playing Michael tough during the 1992-93 six-game Knicks-Bulls Eastern Conference finals clash. In fact, for the first two games at Madison Square Garden, Starks held the upper hand. In the end, though, even the boastful Starks knew the real winner.

"All you can do is try to make him work as hard as you can on both ends of the floor and try to tire him out," Starks says. "All you can do is try to get up on him and take him out of his game as much as possible."

No Answers

The only true way to stop Jordan was to not let him into the arena. If he was lost among a forest of arms in the paint, Michael somehow managed to get off a shot. If a defense forced him outside, he'd gladly pull up and nail a three-pointer. If he was fouled, he'd coolly knock down every free throw awarded him.

Majerle seemed best suited to at least keep Jordan at a reasonable pace in the 1992-93 Finals. Thunder Dan, also 6-6 and at least 20 pounds heavier than Jordan, is a defensive wizard well-accustomed to being assigned to cover an opponent's best scorer.

But . . . "He has no weaknesses," Majerle said after the decisive Game 6. "You can't play him to drive, you can't play him for his jump shot, and you can't shade him to his right or left. His first step is so quick, you can't keep him from going by you, and you can't play him too tight, or he'll go backdoor on you.

"You just have to make him work hard and do your best. The problem is, most of the time your best just isn't good enough."

That's why Westphal ultimately tried something different, opting for the barely 6-1 Kevin Johnson as the series progressed. The Suns settled for keeping a quicker, shorter player in front of Jordan, and hoped he was worn down enough that his long-range shooting would be erratic. And it was, from time to time. But Michael's will and that uncanny predilection for big plays never ceased.

"Nobody does anything well against Jordan," Westphal says. "He's just going to do whatever he wants on anybody you put out there. Nobody has ever controlled him.

"He misses sometimes, and if he does, a guy can say he played great defense on him. But I can assure you, that guy doesn't have anything to do with it."

Like no other player in sports, Jordan controlled his own destiny every time he stepped onto the court. Whether he simply had another night at the office (his lifetime scoring average is a record 32.3 points per game) or he became Superman and crossed the half-century mark (as he did 34 times during his career), Michael was totally in charge.

And just to rub salt into NBA coaches' wounds, Michael has returned. In his fifth game, Jordan scored 55 points (that's 35 times) to beat the Knicks. Sorry Pat Riley, Mike's officially back.

The only thing that has changed about Michael's game is his jersey number. But don't worry, everyone knows where Jordan is at all times. Trouble is, they still can't do a thing to stop him. •

Mike Kahn covers the NBA for The Morning News Tribune in Tacoma, Wash.

Inspired by the dreams of his late father, who introduced him to baseball as a youngster, Michael set out on an improbable quest after retiring from basketball. He fell short of his goal, but it wasn't for lack of effort.

running do

By Rubin E. Grant

vn a dream

On a July night in 1993 in North Carolina, James Jordan pulled his car to the side of the road to take a nap. Police said two young men came upon him at random to rob him. In the end, they allegedly killed him.

James Jordan wasn't just anybody. He was the father of the world's greatest basketball player — Michael Jordan.

Jordan took the murder of his father, his closest friend, hard. So hard in fact, that three months later he decided to retire from the NBA and pursue his dream of being a baseball player.

The dream actually took root when Michael was 6 years old and his father introduced him to baseball. It was the first sport he played. But the dream fell by the wayside once his wondrous basketball skills became evident, first at North Carolina, later in the NBA.

After Michael led the Chicago Bulls to their first NBA championship in 1991, James Jordan tried to convince his son to leave basketball and launch a baseball career. But Michael wasn't ready to abandon the sport that made him a global figure. His Bulls won two more NBA titles during the next two seasons.

But after his father was murdered, Jordan considered playing baseball one way to honor him. Two months after retiring from the NBA, Jordan started taking cuts in the batting cage underneath Comiskey Park, preparing to be a baseball player. When the news leaked to the media, a predictable frenzy ensued. One Jordan indoor practice session — he took a few cuts and fielded some simple fly balls — turned into a three-ring circus. Jerry Reinsdorf, owner of the White Sox and the Bulls, eventually signed Michael to a minor league contract.

The odyssey began at spring training in Sarasota, Fla., where Jordan faced a legion of critics. A *Sports Illustrated* cover told him to "Bag It." Some former major leaguers said he was disgracing the national pastime. But Jordan remained undaunted.

JIM GUND / ALLSPORT USA

"I tried to keep it hush-hush as much as I could," Jordan says. "I wasn't trying to steal anybody's show. I'm just trying to fulfill my own dream."

In spring training, Jordan looked like someone who hadn't played baseball in 14 years. In 13 exhibition games for the White Sox, he collected just three weak singles in 20 at-bats. Hardly deserving a spot on the roster, Jordan was farmed out to the Double-A Birmingham Barons. Formerly the greatest basketball player in the world, Michael now was a 31-year-old rookie outfielder in the minors, traveling the byways of the South by bus.

Michael made the best of it. He provided the Barons with a luxury bus and tried to fit in as one of the guys while attempting to improve his skills.

Throughout it all, Michael found he wasn't alone on his journey. James Jordan walked with

him every step of the way.

"Every morning, I talk to him subconsciously," Jordan said as he sat one day in the Barons' clubhouse at Hoover Metropolitan Stadium. " 'Keep doing what you're doing,' he'd tell me. 'Keep trying to make it happen. Don't give a damn about the media.' Then he'd say something funny, or recall something about when I was a boy, when we'd be in the backyard playing catch together like we did all the time."

Media from around the world — Germany, Japan, England, Sweden, Israel — flocked to Hoover, a Birmingham suburb, to see Jordan take his swings at baseball. Celebrities such as Kathie Lee Crosby and Kenny Rogers also visited, as did sports superstars Charles Barkley, Cornelius Bennett, Chris Chelios and Chi Chi Rodriguez. Fans came out in record numbers, too. The Barons drew a franchise record 467,867 fans in 1994.

Jordan's teammates enjoyed the aura of excitement Michael brought to the Barons.

"It's been like a party that's never stopped," third baseman Chris Snopek said during the season. "Playing every day in the minor leagues can get boring, but it's not boring with Michael around. He's a big celebrity, and he brought excitement to every park and every city we went to in the league."

Jordan fashioned a 13-game hitting streak the first month of the season. But then opposing pitchers adjusted and started feeding him a steady diet of breaking pitches. His batting average nose-dived below .200 and, despite his sinewy 6-6 frame, he exhibited little power.

Michael didn't hit his first home run until late July. The 380-foot shot came at Hoover Metropolitan Stadium on a 1-1 fastball from Carolina Mudcats reliever Kevin Rychel.

"It's been like a party that's never stopped. He's a big celebrity, and he brought excitement to every park and every city we went to in the league."
— Barons third baseman Chris Snopek on having Michael as a teammate

Jordan's mother, wife, brother and sister were in attendance. As he crossed the plate he pointed to his family in the skybox and then to the heavens to acknowledge his late father.

"Once I saw that pitch, I made a pretty good turn and I hit it really solid. Once I hit it, I knew it was gone," Jordan recalls. "It was a great feeling. My family was happy they were able to see it, and I was happy they were there. They've been supportive of me since I was a kid."

The home run came two days before Jordan's father would have celebrated his 58th birthday.

"That's the best birthday present I could give him," Michael said after his round-tripper. "It still makes me kind of emotional because I wish he were here to see it. But I know he saw it. Once I got across the plate, I just kind of paid tribute to my father. I wanted to point up to him and say, 'That was for you.' "

A late-season surge in which Michael hit above .300 elevated his final batting average to .202. Still, it represented the lowest mark in the Southern League. He finished with three home runs and 51 RBI, and tied for fifth in the league with 30 steals. But he also struck out 114 times in 436 at-bats and committed 11 errors, the most of any outfielder. He also was thrown out 18 times attempting to steal and was picked off several more times.

Through it all, Jordan appeared happy, even content.

"I know people don't believe me when I say this, but I'm having the time of my life," he said. "I'm enjoying this whole experience. I'm getting the opportunity that so few people in life get — a second chance to live out a boyhood dream."

Even so, it clearly was evident Jordan had trouble with the finer points of the game, such as working a pitcher, base running and playing the outfield.

But Michael's competitive fire wouldn't allow him to settle for mediocrity. He was determined to improve. After the Barons' season ended, he went to the Arizona Fall League to enhance his skills. He hit .252, but more

the jordan line

1994 TEAM	G	AB	R	H	2B	3B	HR	RBI	SO	SB	CS	AVG	E
Birmingham (SL)	127	436	46	88	17	1	3	51	114	30	18	.202	11
Scottsdale (AFL)	35	123	24	31	4	1	0	8	16	34	6	.252	2

Key: SL (Double-A Southern League); AFL (Arizona Fall League)

strikeouts (34) than hits (31) in 123 at-bats attested to the work still ahead of him.

Scouts confirmed the daunting nature of his quest.

"If he were 20 years old, you might sign him out of a tryout camp because he's an above-average runner," Detroit scout Dave Roberts said. "But he's got a long swing. He's got a slow bat. He throws well below average. His instincts in the outfield are bad, and he doesn't have any power. He has no explosiveness in his hands.

"You have to be able to recognize a breaking ball, wait and explode on it," he adds. "He doesn't have that, and that's not really something you learn. You're born with it. You don't see a guy who's 6-6 with no power making it."

Still, the White Sox had planned to send Jordan to Triple-A Nashville in 1995. But not long after reporting to spring training, Jordan became disillusioned with baseball's labor problems. He didn't want to be associated with the replacement players, so he tersely ended his one-year baseball experiment.

"As a 32-year-old minor leaguer who lacks the benefit of valuable baseball experience during the past 15 years, I am no longer comfortable that there is meaningful opportunity to continue my improvement at a satisfactory pace," Jordan said in a prepared statement that announced the end of his dream.

But his abandonment of one dream ultimately fulfilled the wildest fantasies of his most ardent admirers — Michael's return to the NBA. •

Rubin E. Grant is a sportswriter for the Birmingham (Ala.) Post-Herald.

"I know people don't believe me when I say this, but I'm having the time of my life. I'm getting the opportunity . . . to live out a boyhood dream."
— Michael on his season in the minors

MICHAEL JORDAN'S

AMAIRIGAN DREAMER

STORY BY JACK DEVRIES

PENCILS BY AL BIGLEY

INKS BY AL BIGLEY

COLOR BY JEFF AMANO AND OMAR MEDIANO

LETTERING BY OMAR MEDIANO

STORY CONSULTANTS:
PEPPER HASTINGS,
JAY JOHNSON, RUDY KLANCNIK

EDITOR: FRED L. REED III

BECKETT® REMEMBERS

Even while temporarily grounded, Michael Jordan remained a favorite subject of *Beckett* readers

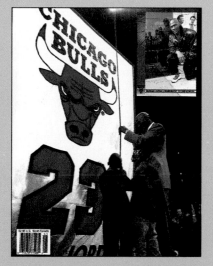

Four months after issue #41 (December 1993) of *Beckett Basketball Monthly* noted his farewell to basketball, Jordan appeared on the cover of *Beckett Baseball Card Monthly* (issue #109/April 1994) getting into the swing of his new career. Little did we know that the retirement gala pictured on the back cover of issue #54 (January 1995) was premature.

C ontrary to popular belief, Michael Jordan didn't create the game of basketball. A doctor named James Naismith deserves credit for that. Michael simply took the sport to a level no one knew existed.

Michael Jordan also wasn't the first basketball star to send collectors scurrying for their piggy banks and sledgehammers. A long list of hoop luminaries preceded Air Jordan's appearance on hardwood and cardboard. Yet from his NBA debut in 1984 to today, no player on the planet meant more to his sport or the hobby than Michael.

It comes as little surprise that Jordan has found a home on more *Beckett Basketball Monthly* covers than any other player.

Cover photos and artwork are but one way to look at this legend, though. *Beckett®* Remembers gives readers an assist in uncovering the man behind the superstar.

M ichael was pictured kissing his brand-new best friend — the world championship trophy — on issue #14 (September 1991).

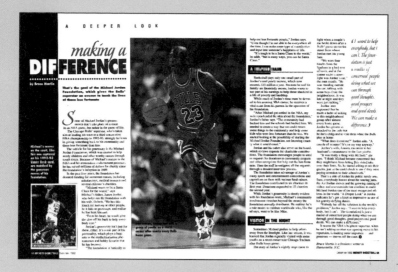

Michael, or at least an artistic representation of him, helped us celebrate a historic issue when he took flight on issue #25 (August 1992).

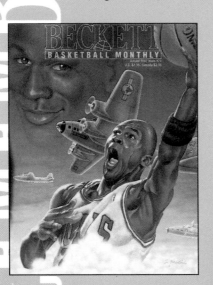

Issue #27 (October 1992) proved Jordan is indeed a work of art.

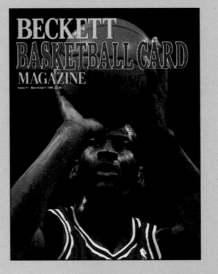

When *Beckett Basketball Monthly* tipped off issue #1 in March 1990, who better to put up the first shot than Mike?

MJ was caught holding up his end of another Olympic dream along with four of his Dream Team sidekicks on issue #24 (July 1992).

Jordan appeared wearing his 1984 United States Olympic team duds on issue #10 (May 1991).

Before the tragic death of his father, James, earlier this year, we focused on the strong bond between the two in issue #23 (June 1992).

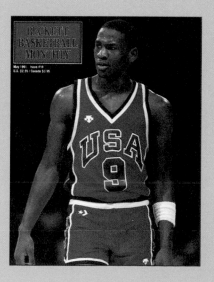

BECKETT GREAT SPORTS HEROES

DON'T MISS THE WHOLE NEW LINEUP!

They are household names, and their performance on the court or field has made them legends. Just a mention of these extraordinary athletes brings to mind the epitome of grace under pressure, courage, persistence, and the highest levels of sportsmanship.

Beckett Publications and House of Collectibles are proud to celebrate the top sports heroes of yesterday, today, and tomorrow with the continuing series of Beckett Great Sports Heroes.

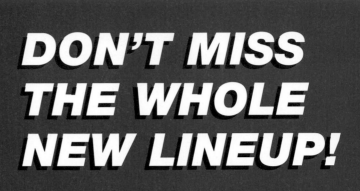

Look for these exciting titles wherever books are sold...